Negative Capability

Marvin Bram

Contents

Keats at Thirty

Cast of Characters

John Keats

Tom Keats

Joseph Severn

Jean-Francois Champollion

Marcel Rogin, *a sixty-year-old Parisian flaneur*

Vivienne Bonnot, *thirty, a brilliant linguist*

Scenes

Act 1, Scene 1

At rise, John lies on a chaise in a sparsely furnished garret. Tom sits opposite.

JOHN

The weight of twice your years
Burdens me, Tom.
As strength returns, my game with death –
Such pain conjoined for most of us with age, not youth –
Is cause to feel excess of age.

TOM
Gently.

Dear brother…
When I tell you what you surely know,
That you're absurdly far from twice my age,
My aim is not to count your years
But to ignore such arid numbers –
As you yourself ignore them in your claim –
And tell you that you're *half* my age,
And half of *that* – a child,
Undiminished by passing time.
You're full in mind
Among these crowds of emptied men.

JOHN
Smiling.

So you *would* say, Tom.

TOM

I, or you, would say…ah, bother.

It's often that we cannot voice our thoughts.
But words have now been said,
Even if in inner silence…

JOHN
Laughing.

…as "upon a peak in Darien?"

TOM
Laughing along.

As upon a peak in Darien.

JOHN

But what is brought to life
By opening the book of mind
To put beside great Homer's lines?

TOM

More than Attic verse and meter, John,
More than Attic warrior force:
The very shape of mind itself,
At birth complete,
Its fate to sing.

Enter Joseph.
Tom rises, stands back.

JOSEPH
Nervously, as if to himself.

Hesitant to leave
Even for a moment,
I feared relapse.

Relieved.

But here you are, your brow returned
To thought, from pain.

JOHN

Which I owe to you, dear friend.

JOSEPH

Not to me. To fortune
And to the span and depth
Of a spirit wounded
But indomitable.

JOHN
Shrugging off Joseph's explanation.

Joseph, Joseph,
Kindness heals.
Your kindly ministrations
Healed the wounds of which you speak
And became a part of
My course of life
Atom by atom.

JOSEPH
Moved.

To become a part of your…

Contemplatively.

John, I think I know
How and when your genius
Grew to such a size
As the world will soon
Announce to constitute
The most complete poetic gift
Mankind has known.

JOHN
Indulgently.

Yes, Joseph.

JOSEPH

It was Tom.

Tom smiles broadly, expresses
amusement, then returns to
serious attention.

JOHN
Gravely.

How I miss him.

JOSEPH
Overcome.

Your grief upon his death…
Your imperious grief…

Gathering himself.

In the heat of many weeks
Ever by his bedside, feeling
Every gasp of breath and wrenching cough,

Exultant.

You wrote *Hyperion.*
As you suffered, you wrote.
As Tom was dying,
You brought his spirit
Into your own, becoming twice
What you had been.
Hyperion became your work and his,
As the Odes would be –

A monument built
By both of you as one.

JOHN

If what you say is true
Then Tom and I will gladly
Share such authorship
As the future brings.

JOSEPH
With deliberation.

I'm put in mind
Of Socrates –
No poet but…

JOHN
Interrupting.

…though philosophizing
Poetizes in its way.

JOSEPH

In its way, of course.
The philosophy to which I refer,
However, does not speak.
Socratic silence
Calls up for me the voice of *"…autumn"*:
Both by doubled minds.
For Socrates would stand in trance
Attending two internal voices,
Simultaneous voices
That spoke his deepest thoughts to him alone.
So much did he distrust
Both speech and writing;
For how could thought, *doubled,*
Suit speech or writing
That utters single words

One after another?

JOHN
Surprised and impressed.

I never knew
How deeply read
In Plato's work you are.
I see your doublings
In Socrates, and if I may –
For I agree I could not lose
And *would* not lose
My brother Tom –
In me.

JOSEPH

I'm compelled to wonder, John,
Whether singularity,
The state that all but you…

JOHN
Laughing.

…and Socrates?

JOSEPH

…that all but you must suffer,
Is deprivation.

JOHN

Singularity deprivation?
It's surely so.
You said "empty men."
They are merely one
When to be complete
Must be to be two in one.
But emptiness is not their choice;

The superficial lives that other ones,
With meager hearts,
Have thrust upon them,
Have drained them dry.
A heart must seek and occupy another heart
That a doubled life might grow.

JOSEPH

We must not despise them, then,
But pity them.

JOHN

Better help than pity,
Eh, my friend?

JOSEPH
Excited.

Yes, to help,
Each as he can.
You, John, in *Hyperion*
And the Odes,
Take each of us
On roads of plangent words and pauses
To our second selves,
There to see as if in undisturbed water,
Ourselves enlarged.

JOHN

Let me say again
That if your tale's
Not made of mist
But has some solidity,
Then poetry,
If not philosophy…

JOSEPH

Interrupting.

…which proceeds beyond philosophy…

JOHN

…well, is not the same,
In all events –
Then perhaps it shares,
With medicine, my first vocation,
The Hippocratic urge:
To heal.

JOSEPH

I assure you, John,
That while you suffered from consumption,
And then in time defeated it,
Your body coming back to you,
My own spirit,
Shrunk at first from worry,
Was healed by verses that you spoke
With at first depleted breath.

JOHN

A type of reciprocity, Joseph?

JOSEPH

No restoration of health
In one direction
Maintains its way
Unless there comes to be
A movement in return.
Restoration, like the mind,
Is a doubling;
Or it remains a deprivation.

John sits up.

JOHN

We see a child, but we do *not,*
For there *is* no "child"
But "the mother and child together."

JOSEPH

I believe there is no "person"
But "the person and much loved friend together."

JOHN

Yes, "and much loved friend."

Rattling at the outer door.

JOSEPH

I'll see who it is.

Joseph exits hurriedly.
Tom resumes his chair.

TOM

Never would I have guessed
That Joseph thinks so well.

JOHN

His cheer and whimsy
Fooled us all.

TOM

Taking you to Rome
Revealed his depth.

JOHN

And *understanding* Rome,
As I did not:
Empire, arms, and law;
Surfaces and the light
We thought were all in all.
But here, in France,
To which he'd gone before,
And understood profoundly:
Not millennia of time
And the classical pulse of Rome,
Shallow in its feeling.
Rather here, in Paris
Nine or ten centuries ago,
The medieval heart of France
Expressed the roots of feeling.
Not arms, argument, and light,
But mystery, art, and shadow.

TOM

Rome was not for you,
It's philosophy seeking light.
Poetry, or may we say,
Wisdom, the same, seeks the dark.
When we cannot see,
We imagine greatly.
Light reveals the fixed and literal,
What the dark reveals is ever-changing,
Forms becoming other forms
As our minds in churning fullness wish.

JOHN

I've become a pilgrim
To a thousand years ago.
There to live upon
The soil of poetry.

> Tom rises and steps back as
> Joseph enters, with Marcel.

JOSEPH

It was Marcel at the door.

JOHN
To Marcel.

I'm glad to see you, Marcel.

MARCEL

And I you, my dear Keats.
I've come with much to tell you.

JOHN

Good. Please sit.

MARCEL
To John and Joseph.

My thanks.
I've been to such a house
Of miracles, my friends,
As I never could imagine.
What I have seen
Will lift your hearts.

JOHN
Laughing.

You make me curious beyond bearing.

JOSEPH
To Marcel.

Let me get you something.

MARCEL
Enthusiastically.

Thank you, no.
You, John, will see it all.
A house in the Rue St. Jacques,
A school, where the deaf
Are taught to make their inner lives
Clear to others without speech.
A miraculous place,
For silence –
With hands and face in rapid,
Wondrous gesture –
Proves to say more than words,
I think, can say.
More than words, gentlemen.

JOSEPH
Impatiently.

You speak to the master of the word, Rogin.

JOHN

Wait, dear Joseph, wait.
Marcel comes in good spirit,
His news a marvel.

To Marcel.

How more than words, Marcel?

MARCEL

Let me take a step
Back to Bonaparte's Egyptian venture.
The signs he found,
The silent hieroglyphs,
In principle divorced from sound,
Each, I now am certain, contains
A cornucopia, gentlemen:
Meanings pouring forth

As long as one might contemplate the sign.
The mind fills…

JOSEPH
To Marcel.

"Fills," is it?

MARCEL

Exorbitantly, Severn;
A plenitude of meaning.

JOHN
Increasingly, almost dangerously excited.

By the gods…

MARCEL

What it is I come to say is this:
The gestures made by hands and face
In the Rue St. Jacques,
Like the emblems
Carved in high relief
Beside the Sphinx,
Offer *their* plenitudes in silence.

JOHN

How came such a thing to be?

MARCEL

Aware of your boundless sympathy,
Nothing could please me more than to tell you
Whence the miracle comes.
It's not from dry instruction,
Not from quiet rumination,
Nor from Christian inspiration; but

From the poor and wild young of Paris,
Who, deaf, despised, long ago created
Their own effective "speech,"
The speech of hands.
The Rue St. Jacques has made
Of this a matter to be taught
To those who do not know it,
And indeed, I think, to such as hear
But think the hands can complement the voice;
For everyone, perhaps, would flourish
Knowing what only Egypt knew...

JOHN
Almost overcome.

Egypt and the poor…
Neither wealth nor genius
Has granted such a gift to humankind
As these children have –
By bravely claiming their right
To live as human beings.

JOSEPH
Concerned for John.

It's a wonder, John, certainly.
But the time has come
For you to rest.
Marcel and I will leave you now.
Quiet your mind
And rest.

MARCEL

Good day, then, Keats.
This has been enough – a
Taxing visit, perhaps,
Requiring assimilation.

JOHN

Yes, I'll rest.
I'll rest.

Joseph makes sure that John
is comfortable, then he and
Marcel leave quietly. Tom
approaches John.

TOM

A new day.

JOHN

Indeed it is.
Even now I sense
A new beginning.
I have wondered,
What can I be to Shakespeare?
What he to me?
I believe I soon will know.

John and Tom doze
in their places.
Blackout.
Joseph enters very
quietly,
but John and Tom
hear him.
Tom rises, stands back.

JOSEPH

Ah, I'm sorry, John.
I'd planned to leave the letter
By your bed.

JOHN

I'm always glad to see you, Joseph.
Besides, I sleep too much.

JOSEPH

There's healing done in sleep, I think.

JOHN

Perhaps, but time may not be with me.
I must write.

JOSEPH

Then I interrupt too much.

JOHN

True of everyone but you.
You forget your gift to me
Of every moment
Since I nearly died in Rome.

Cheerfully.

Interrupt at will.
And now, the letter.

JOSEPH
Hesitatingly.

From Fanny Brawne.

JOHN
Eagerly, but with consternation.

Let me see it.

John reads.

She says she does not
Understand why it is we stay.

JOSEPH

May I say more of her
Than has been my habit?
I never wished –
I never will wish –
To trouble you with idle talk.
I've thought these months
On shore, on sea,
In Rome, and here,
Of your place in man's career.
I think in awe
Of your preeminence.

JOHN
Concerned.

You have a larger life
Than this with me.
In this much concentrated space
Which calls on you for so much thought of me,
Do not surrender your hopes
Apart from me.

JOSEPH

I will not.
I assure you that I've not
Over-estimated your worth.
That cannot be done.
It's a sober friend I can assure you
Who measures what he says
Against an over-riding wish
To speed you back to writing,
Restored to health, when, let me add,
I will have more than time enough
To fulfill my hopes.

JOHN

What can I say?
Trusting your circumspection, then,
Tell me, Joseph –
Fanny…

JOSEPH

You were…over-mastered, John,
By impulse.
Miss Brawne is and will remain
Moved to and fro herself by impulse.
But what for you was passing,
In her will never change.
For that brief time, you see,
You were in fact alike.
You are now another person.
You say, "circumspection."
Mine is a simple kind compared
To what will come to you,
Comprehending every inner fact –

With heat.

No, exposing inner facts
Not before discernable,
No, adding inner facts to mankind's store.

More calmly.

She will never see you
As you are,
And unseen, you will chafe.
But loyal and determined to obliterate
Your yearning to be seen,
You will stay with her.
Never let that happen.
Never, I beg.

JOHN
Abstractedly.

I hear every word
But I'm confused.
Do I not love her?

JOSEPH

Impulse of youth
Is always called
And wrongly called: love.

JOHN

Advise me, Joseph.

JOSEPH

Let some months go by,
Here, in Paris.
You will grow,
She will not.
Each will understand the other,
In time,
And you will go your different ways.
The reasons to converge
Are passed.
The reasons to diverge instead,
Will multiply.

JOHN

Paris has become a refuge for us,
These twisting streets and ancient stones.
The shadows of which you've spoken
Are harbors into which
Ghostly ships arrive and stay,
Awaiting me to plumb their holds.

How it may become
For her and me?
We'll wait, and see.

Act 1, Scene 2

Joseph and Marcel sit at a table outside a small restaurant on the Rue St. Jacques.

MARCEL

To think that Keats was near
His death at twenty-five.
He'd barely launched his life in art.

JOSEPH

He'd found his art
A year before his health gave way.
From one autumn to the next
He wrote the greatest lyrics yet composed .

MARCEL
Inspired.

When you kindly brought the Odes to me
I felt at once the rarest joy,
An elevation to a sphere
That knows no measured time or bordered space.
To lift a fellow man to such a place…

JOSEPH

…to lift the world itself.

MARCEL

Is he happy, Severn?

JOSEPH

He lives when he writes.
At other times he sucks up more
Of what he finds around him
Than anyone can fathom.

MARCEL

A "more" that comprehends
Both what can serve
And what can wreck him?

JOSEPH

You've sensed the problem rightly.
Keats is loath to push away
Even what will weaken him.

MARCEL

It's difficult when young
To know what *gives* to one
And the opposite, what *steals* from one.
His judgment will mature.

JOSEPH

Of course it will.
Until that time, his happiness
Will lie with poetry alone.

MARCEL

I can but infer
From hints that you and he
Have inadvertently let slip
That a woman comes between
Dear Keats and happiness.

JOSEPH

As often is the case,
The remedy *appears* to be
The joining of the two
Whom circumstance
Has separated.
It's immaturity
Of judgment to think
That such conjoining
Will bring the happiness so dearly sought.
No, to wait is best.

MARCEL

Well, young man,
There's more than that to say.
To wait: perhaps.
But what of empty waiting?

JOSEPH

Not so for Keats.
He'll write.

MARCEL

Yes, he'll write.
But don't you want
Ecstasies of other kinds for him?

JOSEPH

Of course I do.

MARCEL

Perhaps the woman whom
You see a danger to him
Can be displaced.

Great spirits come to us
In skirts as well as britches, Severn.
Our Voltaire knew this perfectly,
And flourished best
When in company with a woman
His equal in perspicacity.

JOSEPH

We in Britain
Little think of women thus.
Assertion stays with men.
Great achievement comes from us.
Is that not so in France?

MARCEL

Largely yes, it's so.
Exceptions, though,
Are scarcely few.
Away from academic study,
Which remains a male preserve,
The salon, the space of women,
Scintillates with thought.
I myself would never lapse attendance,
So stimulating are salon nights.

JOSEPH

I'm astonished, Rogin.

MARCEL

A splendid woman,
Vivienne Bonnot,
Versed in English,
And German, too,
Has more than sung
Sweet praise of Keats;
She has understood him.

Her soul and his
Are tuned alike.
Each can dwell
In another's thoughts,
And look upon
The other's vista.

JOSEPH

Marcel, have you prepared an argument?
Does this Vivienne Bonnot
Aspire to meet our friend?

MARCEL

Mademoiselle Bonnot –
Good Vivienne –
Only she can match our friend,
Not in composition
But in kindness.
So she will not presume.

JOSEPH

It's you, I see, who wishes
Keats and her to meet.

MARCEL

I think perhaps our John
Has had surfeit of girls.
As large a mind as Keats commands,
Recognition by a woman, not a girl,
Giving back to him
A woman's gift,
Will warm that mind
And keep him glad
To meet each day.

JOSEPH

Can any other,
Man or woman,
Bring to Keats
A view of things
Unknown to him?

MARCEL

One sets one's vision forward
Or to the side –
Never everywhere at once.
It can't be done.
A woman looks
Where men do not,
And looks with woman's eyes.

JOSEPH

You say that Keats
Allied with someone,
A woman…

MARCEL
Interrupting.

…whose judgment is commodious…

JOSEPH

…might give to Keats
The full circumference
To which you refer.

MARCEL

I do.

JOSEPH

I'll contemplate
The possibility.
It's up to him, however.
It's Keats who'll choose
To know whomever he wants to know.

MARCEL
Laughing.

If Keats is asked
By me, perhaps, to see her,
He'll not refuse:
His kindness will not permit it.
But she would not presume:
Her kindness will not permit it.
So rest at ease, my boy.
They'll never meet.

Act 2, Scene 1

Vivienne and Marcel sit at the same table outside the restaurant on the Rue St. Jacques on the following day.

VIVIENNE
Overwrought.

Ah, Marcel, I hope
You didn't approach him
On my account.
I would die before
Delaying his recovery.

MARCEL
Reassuringly.

No no, Vivienne.
It was Severn I approached –
A most protective friend to Keats,
In fact, a barrier
Of some dimension.

VIVIENNE
More calmly.

I'm glad he has a friend
So obstinate.
In Severn's place,
I'd find it in myself
To be a martinet.

MARCEL
Laughing.

Indeed: you would have built
A wall no interloper dared to climb.
Would you have barred yourself?

VIVIENNE

A paradox, Marcel.
As his friend, I'd *have*
His company.
It's others I would keep from him.

MARCEL

Vivienne, I must adopt
A more severe position.
It's only good that you
Would bring to him; I know this,
Though you do not.
Defer to me, dear woman.

VIVIENNE
Upset.

Let us talk of something else, Marcel.

MARCEL

I apologize, Mademoiselle.
I'd be very sorry
To offend you.

VIVIENNE
Warmly.

You've not offended me.
I must simply think awhile
About our meeting, Keats and I.
But you and I have more to think about.
You brought Sicard to his attention?

MARCEL

I did, to both of them.
I spoke with heartfelt admiration
Of brilliant work his school has done
With many struck with silence.

VIVIENNE

And of his limits, as you put it?

MARCEL

It's you who thinks
Sicard's conviction that the deaf
Can only walk a certain distance
On the road they wish to travel –
That such a judgment is incorrect.
I agree with him.

VIVIENNE

A great achievement
Can include a great mistake, Marcel.
His is that the deaf
Can never reach the full
Humanity of those who hear.

MARCEL

You believe they can.

VIVIENNE

I know it.
Remember Condillac.
He wrote of this.
A silent language
Of hands and face, he wrote,

Could be, as I recall his phrase,
"A language of copresent thoughts."
We can't comprehend this thing;
If one among us all
Can grasp the consequence
Of Condillac's assertion,
It will be Keats.

MARCEL

I touched upon it:
The force of hands,
Like the force of hieroglyphs,
Creating plenitudes.
Keats was moved.

VIVIENNE

Of course he was.
Still, to hear such things described
Can not compare with
Intimate experience of them.
He has not learned – not yet learned –
The signs of hands and face;
Nor the signs of ancient Egypt.

MARCEL

I wonder if
He'll take them up.

VIVIENNE

He will.
Until that time,
There's something you must do.

MARCEL

I'm at your service, Vivienne.

VIVIENNE

Take Keats to Notre Dame
When Perotin is being sung.

MARCEL
Enthusiastically.

The great motets!
Who else but you could
Join Sicard to Bonaparte and counterpoint –
The signs of flying hands to those of Egypt's scribes –
In the nave of Notre Dame,
Where different texts
Are put to different tunes –
To be performed at once.

VIVIENNE

Everyone believes
That modern ears reject
Such simultaneity.
But Perotin, so long ago,
Assumed a wide reception
Both of words and tones,
Enfolding every strand of thought and feeling.
And more than hearing all of this,
Hearing in between those lines,
The unheard thoughts,
The tones not sung.

MARCEL

What minds they had
When Notre Dame was built.

VIVIENNE
Firmly.

We have them still,
But half of mind now sleeps.

MARCEL

You're telling me
That Keats, awake,
Will hear it all.

VIVIENNE

He will.
And Perotin's motets,
The silent gestures of the deaf,
And Egypt's hieroglyphs,
Finding homes in him,
Will, like seeds,
Ripen into masterworks
Of which humanity
Can only dream.

MARCEL

I will take him there,
And tell him
Whose advice I follow.

VIVIENNE

No, Marcel.
We act for him,
Not for me.

MARCEL

I act for both.

Perotin's polytextual
motets are played
between Scenes 1

and 2 – if possible,
slowed by
half and in English.

Act 2, Scene 2

The garret. John and Tom walk slowly about.

JOHN

This letter, Tom,
How am I to think about it?
How shall I regard its judgments?
More than courtesy informs it, surely.

TOM

And more than elevated taste.
To place your work so firmly in
The tale of human strivings…
Listen once again to what she writes:

"This is not a moment, dear Mister Keats,
Merely in the history of your or our literatures,
Or indeed of literature itself.
This is a moment in the history of humanity.
Champollion is here, now,
Unconcealing the mind of ancient Egypt –
Not "another language,"
But another *kind* of language.
Sicard is here, now,
Unconcealing the minds of those
Who cannot hear –
Again, another *kind* of language.
Notre Dame is here,
Where counterpoint and words are joined together.
And my dear Mister Keats,
You are here, alone equipped
To gather all of this and make them one.

Remain with us, I beg you."

JOHN

Her enthusiasm takes one's breath.

TOM

Fanny writes to importune you home.
Her plan for married life
Requires you home.
Mademoiselle Bonnot writes
To importune you stay.
Humanity, she says, requires that
You join Champollion, Sicard, and Perotin,
To synthesize and add to them
Your growing powers.
To whom is your debt greater?

JOHN

A flesh and blood woman, Tom,
And this but a letter.

TOM

Then you must confront
The flesh and blood author of the letter.

JOHN

Will she visit me here?
I've little stamina.

TOM

Hearing Perotin's motets
In Notre Dame with Marcel
Brought the threat of dire symptoms…

JOHN
Ecstatically.

But a revelation, Tom!
The meaning of a line,
The meaning of a *second* line
Cemented to the first:
A third, *larger* meaning –
A third!
The threat was real,
But I survive with larger purpose.

TOM

Then the game's a great one, dear brother.
Write to her.

Joseph enters.
Tom stands back.

JOSEPH
Smiling.

I thought you promised me
Recumbancy, you villain.

John lies down.

JOHN

There, an honest man again.

JOSEPH

You've thought about the letter?

JOHN

I have.

JOSEPH

Will you see her?

JOHN

If she will see me.

JOSEPH

Then I remove objection.

JOHN

Thank you, Joseph.

JOSEPH
Cheerfully resigned.

Marcel speaks well of her.
She hadn't wished to see you
Before this, fearing she'd disturb you.
She overcame her diffidence
Fearing that you'll leave for England
Before she had a chance to make her case.
Besides, Marcel is sure
A female friend will do you good.

JOHN
Laughing.

Marcel's a jolly fellow.
Female friend…well.

JOSEPH

Someone else to talk to, at least.
A person of appreciable substance.

JOHN
Wryly.

I'm glad to hear you grant
Such substance to a woman –
With inflated views of me.

JOSEPH

There you're wrong, my over-modest friend.
What she says is true.
It's because of that, her letter's truth,
That I object no longer.

JOHN

I hope to justify
Your confidence in me,
Joseph – and hers.

Act 2, Scene 3

The garret a week later. Vivienne sits in a chair next to John, who lies propped up in bed. Tom stands near them.

JOHN

I'm grateful to you for coming here,
Mademoiselle Bonnot.

VIVIENNE

I would need to have
Your poet's genius, Mister Keats,
To tell you of the honor I feel
To be allowed to sit beside you.
If your habit were
To hold your court at the Pole,
And you bade me come,
I'd go forthwith.

JOHN
Laughing.

I was ready to apologize the more
For your traversal of the city,
But you assure me that
The Pole itself is not too far,
So I rest content, having
Spared you frozen seas and angry gales.

VIVIENNE
Cheerfully.

There you are –

My coming a mere nothing.

JOHN
Seriously.

Far from that.
Far from it.
Your kindness is a wonder.
Your letter…

VIVIENNE

Oh, Mister Keats,
It's I who live in wonder of you.
Each time I read your Odes
My eyes and ears,
The tips of my fingers,
My very heart
Are rendered open to wonder,
To all sensation, pain, and pleasure
As they had never before been open.
I am on reading newly born.

JOHN
Stirred.

You say that honor
Is conferred on you
That we speak here,
But what honor it is for me
To think that poems of mine
Affect you as I would hope they might.
My life is justified –
To be for another
What you say I am for you.

VIVIENNE
Putting her hand on John's arm.

Then be justified.

They are immobile for a
long moment.

JOHN

I must know more about you.

VIVIENNE

More about me…
Let me think.
I've long been struck by language.
I've asked myself repeatedly
How words concatenated
Select from secret thoughts,
Against our will as well as with it,
What will emerge into public spheres.
Some have said that everything we think
Can be so moved. I doubted this.
I took to languages so I might find the truth.

JOHN

An ancient question, Mademoiselle,
Whether words record everything we think.
I'm no less absorbed with it.
I have, til now, believed that what you doubt
Is in fact beyond doubt.
Does not the poet transmute inner speech,
Both formed and seeming-formless inner speech,
Into what we hear and understand,
And *to* which we can speak in turn?

VIVIENNE

Could not some of inner speech
Disguise those stirrings often felt
To live apart from speech entirely?

JOHN

Contemplatively.

Perhaps. Perhaps.
My friends more versed in instrumental music
Imply that words can't reach
All depths of inner life,
Allowing Mozart access
To stirrings such as those you name.

VIVIENNE

My correspondent Thomas Young,
Upon whose work the great Champollion has built,
Suggests to me, implicitly, that Mozart's string quintets
Resemble hieroglyphs:
They take us with them
To inner worlds inaccessible
To modern speech and modern script.

JOHN

Your wish that I become
A pupil of Champollion…

Firmly.

I've thought of little else
Since your letter came to me.
I will, dear Mademoiselle,
Beg Champollion to take me as his student.
And to please you further,
I'll add pursuit of Mozart, beyond need of words,
To attendance on Perotin's motets, replete with words.
I remain in Paris.

VIVIENNE
Elated.

What joy you bring us!

JOHN

I'd hoped for many months
That I might rest from poetry,
And instead resume my education.
I felt a lack of readiness
To begin my larger work.
But at the same time,
I thought, In what does education
Consist for me?
Mademoiselle, to you I owe my answer.
I've found my university.

VIVIENNE
Breathlessly.

I'll speak to Champollion in Grenoble.
His English lacks no subtlety;
If he has not as yet
Devoured your work, he will.
He'll then insist on
Passing on to you
Everything he takes
From the Rosetta Stone.
I'll see Sicard tonight.
I'll be indefatigable in your service,
Dear Mister Keats.

                                        They clasp hands.

JOHN

You've renewed my strength.

VIVIENNE

I'll go now.
My strength, too, renewed.

Act 2, Scene 4

The garret two weeks later. John sits in a chair; Champollion sits opposite. An easel half-faces John, half the audience. A large, square, white board sits on the easel, on the tray of which are several colored pastels. Tom stands back.

JOHN
Reflecting.

You tell me, Monsieur Champollion,
That symbolism performs its functions
In ways more subtle…

CHAMPOLLION

…and more different…

JOHN

…more subtle *and* more different
Than I – or you – before imagined.
Is poetry as it stands
Then compromised?

CHAMPOLLION

You wish assurance, Mister Keats.
I cannot give it.
Poetry is compromised.

JOHN

I'm alarmed to hear you say it.

CHAMPOLLION

Perhaps I spoke incautiously.
It's better to say
That poetry *was* compromised,
Long ago, and so, alas, it remains.

JOHN

How, Monsieur?

CHAMPOLLION

The difference to which I referred:
What we call a symbol holds a place for something else,
One and only one other thing.
A useful, arithmetical notion.
Or, contrariwise, a symbol *gathers* meanings to itself
To give to us in turn.
A noble, poetical notion –
The poetical notion,
Eh, Mister Keats?

JOHN
Following closely.

Indeed.

CHAMPOLLION

Egyptian hieroglyphs
Are of the latter kind.
But words set down in *alphabetic* scripts,
The scripts of all the nations save ancient China,
Stand each for one thing only…

JOHN

…for spoken words.

CHAMPOLLION

For spoken words
Which themselves refer
To single things, not many things:
Written "John Keats" to
Spoken "John Keats" to
You and you alone.

JOHN

And a written hieroglyph
To a spoken hieroglyph?

Champollion rises, paces,
but is careful to direct
himself to John.

CHAMPOLLION

Hieroglyphs are never spoken.
Because they mean so much at once
They *can't* be spoken.
They're silent, to be sure,
But *this* silence…fills.

JOHN

Mademoiselle Bonnot
Refers to plenitudes,
To silence, and the eye, not the ear.

CHAMPOLLION

Yes. Rather than precision,
Singularity…

JOHN
Interrupting.

"Singularity," you say.

Pausing.

Ah, I beg your pardon.
Please go on.

CHAMPOLLION

Singularity,
Speech, and the ear –
Which, I add, together mark the time of clocks,
As one spoken word after another
Ticks and ticks again, ad infinitum –
Rather than singularity
We have plenitude,

Portentously.

And in plenitude, *time…stops.*

JOHN
Moved.

In a plenum
There is no time…

CHAMPOLLION

Hieroglyphic writing
Has no past or future tense, Mister Keats.
The world in all its parts and processes,
In all the fullness from which we
In modern days take but a part,
Is concentrated in the present moment
And it remains…in the present moment.
Single meanings give us time and death.
Many meanings lift these curses from us.
Our choice is…

JOHN

Interrupting again.

Precision or plenitude.

CHAMPOLLION

Yes!

JOHN

I hear these things you say,
And say such things myself,
To myself, but hypocritically.
I've no experience of truly what it is
To which you refer.

Champollion places
himself by the easel,
takes up a pastel,
and draws.

CHAMPOLLION

Regard a circle, Mister Keats.
Now draw a horizontal diameter:
It cuts the circle twice,
At eastern and western points.
Draw a vertical diameter:
It also cuts the circle twice,
At northern and southern points.

JOHN

Yes, Monsieur.
The circle is cut in quadrants.

CHAMPOLLION
Gesturing animatedly toward the easel.

Splendid, splendid.

What *are* these quarters
To readers of this hieroglyph?
They signify, at once,
The rooms of the reader's house,
The regions of his village,
And the quadrature of heaven,
All in harmony, each with the other two.

Quickly sketching.

Now draw a hawk at the eastern point,
A mountain in the south,
A ram in the west,
A fire in the north…

JOHN

A stunning picture…

CHAMPOLLION

…a *storied* picture:
The hawk at sunrise, birth;
The ram at sunset, death;
The mountain is endurance;
The fire dissolution.
To each direction
Adheres a hundred stories.
Why should one depart
From such a symbol
To another one?
Remain before it, rather.
One's mind and life then fill;
Time comes to a halt
In this plenum.

JOHN
Intensely.

A single hieroglyph?

CHAMPOLLION

Yes! Yes!

John rises unsteadily.

JOHN
As if a revelation.

Each hieroglyph…each one… a poem?

CHAMPOLLION
Smiling broadly.

You understand me exactly.

Slowly John sits.

JOHN

The voice supplanted silence –
When?

CHAMPOLLION

Twenty, perhaps thirty centuries ago.

JOHN

And since, you think?

CHAMPOLLION

Very little poetry,
Quite against the world's opinion.
You, Mister Keats,
Chaucer, Spencer, Shakespeare, Milton:
Is that enough in English,
When all are starved for plenitude?

JOHN

Poetry, then, must overcome
An absence and a presence:
The absence of a symbolism that gathers meaning –
Of hieroglyphic fullness.
And the presence of a symbolism that merely substitutes –
The alphabets and their often empty voices.

CHAMPOLLION

A double overcoming.
Precisely put.

JOHN

Has Mademoiselle Bonnot
Discussed Sicard with you?

CHAMPOLLION

Yes. Enthralling work.

JOHN

Your best opinion:
Can silent gestures duplicate
What hieroglyphs present to us?

CHAMPOLLION

I think they can.
No, I know it.

JOHN
As if to himself.

Egyptian can never be my language
Of composition;

The gestures of the deaf
Cannot be written down.
What shall I do
With what I know a poem might be?

John rises, approaches
Champollion, shakes
his hand.

Shall I see you next week, Monsieur?

CHAMPOLLION
Smiling.

With paints and brushes, Mister Keats.
We'll draw and color hieroglyphs
With greater permanence than this.
It's thus you'll have experience
Of plenitude through line and tint;
And since it's work of hands and eye,
Perhaps this other work of hands,
Sicard's appropriation of the means
Our urchins of the streets who cannot speak
Make themselves clear and more than clear
One to another –
Perhaps this other work of hands
May disclose its role in future poetry.

Champollion exits. John
sits.

Act 3, Scene 1

Joseph's sitting room, London, 1825. A small table and four chairs stand downstage left. It is mid-afternoon. John and Joseph walk slowly about the room. Tom stands back.

JOSEPH

Good news, I think.

JOHN

Yes. Certainly.
I suppose so.

JOSEPH

Suppose?

JOHN

We were once engaged.

JOSEPH

When young and stupid.

JOHN
Laughing.

Yes.

JOSEPH

You want her happy.

JOHN

I do.

JOSEPH

Fanny is shallow, if vivacious.
"A minx," you said back then.
Durant is shallow too, and stodgy –
A perfect complement.

JOHN

You're likely right.
It's only that I sometimes think
Myself disloyal…
These nearly five years gone…

JOSEPH

Glorious years in Paris, John.
Your letters to her explained
Your life with Vivienne
And your "education" as you called it,
Not omitting your hopes when you returned to England:
She understood nothing of it.
Now you're back,
And Fanny's married well.
Not a history of disloyalty, I think,
But of fulfillment.

JOHN

At all events,
Vivienne and I are here.

JOSEPH
Laughing.

Your sister can not contain herself.

JOHN

And my brother George returns
With Georgiana.
The time has come
At last for us to live
In call of one another.

JOSEPH

The time at last:
The time of restoration.
The strength of English drama
Soon to be restored.

Aware of the hour.

Oh, the time indeed;
I must run off.

JOHN

My thanks for coming, Joseph.
You represent my continuity –
London to Rome, Rome to Paris, Paris home.
How true a friend you've been.

JOSEPH

And you to me, and you to me.

John and Joseph shake
hands.
Joseph exits.
Tom steps forward.

JOHN
Pondering.

The time at last, he said.

TOM

You're ready.

JOHN

Am I?

TOM

Of course you are.
You kept your Shakespeare with you
And pondered volume after volume.
You know him best of all who've known him.

JOHN

And now?

TOM

You and he together rise
To drama that reveals
The depths of human feeling
Hitherto concealed.
And more: that draws from all
Who hear and see your work
Intensities. "Soul-making," John,
Remember?

JOHN
As if to himself.

The vale of soul-making…

TOM

Champollion proved to you
That greater fullness than you dreamt
Of thought and feeling and unnamed states of mind
Was known to humankind and can be known again.

JOHN

Undeniable proof.

TOM

Sicard proved to you
That certain gestures reproduce
Effects Egyptian hieroglyphs express.

JOHN
Increasingly animated.

And gesture can be *seen*...

TOM

On a stage,
Your stage.

JOHN

My actors...
Will they sign and speak at once?
Can sounds and meanings
Borne by spoken words and *heard*
Join such gestures, *seen,*
And make my meanings larger?

TOM

Why may not their signs
Enthrall the eye while their words
Enthrall the ear?

A counterpoint of meanings.

JOHN

A new music.

Act 3, Scene 2

Joseph's sitting room later the same day. A full decanter and four wine glasses have appeared on the table, along with a sheaf of blank sheets, pens, and an inkwell. John strides back and forth, lost in thought. Tom stands apart. Vivienne and Marcel enter.

VIVIENNE
Happily.

A friend has come to see us, John.

> Vivienne kisses John.
> John and Marcel
> embrace.

JOHN

Marcel! How good of you
To make the journey.

MARCEL

For you and lovely Vivienne, anything.
I said to myself, Marcel,
Betake your indolent self across the Channel.
How can Keats arrange his affairs without your help,
Eh, Marcel, you dog?

VIVIENNE
To John.

Darling Marcel implored me
To tell him frankly whether
Your work and spirits
Were such that a visit from him
Would not tax you.

As always, the heart of kindness
Behind the flaneur's mask.

MARCEL
Theatrically.

Calumny. Pure, intended calumny.
That you should entertain
The smallest possibility
That motives other than those
Of self-regard can drive me,
Shocks me to the quick.

JOHN

Do sit, old friend.
Take wine with us
And report the news of Paris.

The three sit at the table.
Marcel pours himself a
glass of wine.

MARCEL

Sicard may miss your company
Even more than Champollion does.

JOHN

I was merely their student.

MARCEL

You were never "merely" anything, my boy.
John Keats one's student…hm!

JOHN

I confess to missing them,

Their wisdom and forbearance.

MARCEL

I'd walk with Sicard
To your and Severn's digs
Twice and more each week.
We'd leave a wedge of silent children
Signing at your door.
He would often speak to me
Of your magnetic presence.

JOHN

To learn to sign from him is more than learning.
One's inner life acquires softness
And size and receptivity
That seem to come by night, of themselves.
Sicard's instruction may be of signs;
The consequence feels much like moral growth.

VIVIENNE
To John.

He talked to me in just those terms
About your person and poetry.

MARCEL

Each of you became
The curriculum of the other.
A most unusual friendship.

JOHN

I write to him tonight, Marcel.

VIVIENNE
To Marcel.

And Champollion?

MARCEL

Learning tongues a mile a minute.
I've never heard of most of them.

To John.

Unlike Sicard, he owns a concrete record
Of your weekly sessions –
Shall I say, bespattered with paint?

JOHN
Laughing.

Half our hieroglyphic exercises!
The other half, my own.
I treasure it.

MARCEL

I marvel at you Anglo-Saxons.
That a hieroglyphic emblem
Allows a transmutation
Is no surprise to those of us
In Catholic France – I say
Catholic *France...*

Mumbling.

...let the Vatican...

VIVIENNE
Quickly, laughing.

Yes, yes, Marcel, we understand.

MARCEL

…as I was saying,
Those of us
In Catholic France who enter
Cathedral spaces, buoyed up
By light unknown beyond their walls,
And wholly live the Eucharist.
Transubstantiation, my boy.

JOHN

The Church of England…

MARCEL
Interrupting.

Flut, "the Church of England."
You English mew about –
Not John Keats, I rush to say –
In muddy lanes, expressionless,
Literal, and half asleep.
The modern Englishman and old Egyptian
Occupy antipodes –
If that's the word I want.

VIVIENNE
Laughing.

You're harsh, Marcel.

MARCEL

Flut, Protestants!
They'll bore themselves to death.

JOHN
Smiling, pseudo-portentously.

I rise to defend my countrymen.

MARCEL

Defend your English language, rather.
A splendid language, a doltish people.

VIVIENNE

If you're through, my dear…

MARCEL

Vivienne, my darling,
I slash my wrists before offending you…

VIVIENNE
Continuously amused.

…or John, I'm sure.

MARCEL

Either of you, precious ones,
Either of you.
I wish you happiness…

As if to himself.

…in this sodden country.

JOHN

How long will you remain?

MARCEL

Some weeks, in self-duress, I think.
I plan to stroll your cities
Recording my impressions.
I expect considerable interest

In my memoirs –
When I get around to them.

VIVIENNE

You'll visit us often.

MARCEL

When in London,
I glue myself to you.
You'll beg me to depart.

JOHN
Laughing, but earnestly.

Never, Marcel.

MARCEL

Then to prove your youthful constancy,
Have supper with me tonight
At my redoubt in Piccadilly.

VIVIENNE

Of course we will…John?

JOHN

We descend on you at nine.

MARCEL

Then good day 'til nine.

They rise, embrace.
Marcel exits.
Vivienne and John sit.

JOHN

As fine a fellow as I know.

VIVIENNE

The most resourceful of friends,
A Hermes for us in Paris…
Now perhaps you'll sleep 'til...

JOHN
Agitated.

No, Vivienne.
I'm aswarm with thoughts
Of you in England now, away from Paris;
Of my returning home so changed;
Of drama built on new assumptions
Of what an actor can achieve
And what an audience can accept…

John rises, paces.

And dear Vivienne,
I have no subject.

VIVIENNE

Do set your mind at ease
With regard to me, at least.
You know what life with you
Has done for me.
I feel surplus of life
Each day because
You lie beside me.

John sits.

JOHN

Your home in Paris…

VIVIENNE

You're my home –
Not Paris, not London,
Nor any place without you
Could be my home.

JOHN

You're kind to say so.

VIVIENNE

And Paris, John?
As a child of Revolution
I tire of its course in Paris.
Babeuf was hung because he wanted
France to redistribute wealth
So that the poor might live
As human beings.

Heatedly.

The poor abandoned yet again
While new pretenders climbed their ladders
To wealth and power.

JOHN

The forces that oppress the poor
Design their grievous hurts
Away from observation by their victims.

VIVIENNE

Yet it was the poor of Paris

Who first sustained the Revolution,
In vain anticipation of relief.
But our burghers wanted all impediments
To increase of their wealth removed;
In that they triumphed.

JOHN

Ignoble triumph.

VIVIENNE

Here, in your United Kingdom,
I sense that something new begins to stir.
The owner of a factory, Robert Owen,
Thinks to elevate his workers,
To make them owners too.

JOHN

I've heard of Owen…
The world has seemed to me
To offer too few ways
For men and women to thrive together.
Owen's plan is new, exactly as you say:
From one who owns while many work,
To many who both own and work…

With increasing energy.

Genuinely…new.

Tom attends John
carefully.

VIVIENNE
Noticing.

John?

JOHN

A *subject,* Vivienne.

Excitedly.

Why draw from Greece or Rome
Or fairyland?
Why choose such tales and amplify them?
We live among injustices.
Why must we accept them
When we should and can
Speak out against them?

John rises.

No. Instead a great and English theme,
Worked now to speak for justice.
This island's epic!
But not retold, Vivienne: corrected.
"In our origin lies our end:" it's so.
A new origin, then; a better history.

VIVIENNE
Catching John's fervor.

The Arthurian cycle…

JOHN

Imagine that a mirror image of his story,
Reversed, is told in dramaturgy reconceived.
Cannot the story's content
And its way of being told
Be made anew?

VIVIENNE

Your contrapuntal form
Applied to…

John paces energetically,
as does Vivienne.
Tom begins to place
himself in closer
proximity to John.

JOHN

…a new account of England's origin.
For what has come to us are tales of battles
Little different from struggles fought
By powerful living men
Who want more power still
And relegate the multitudes to themselves.
Arthur defeats a minor king
And then another until he himself becomes high king.

Amused in anticipation of what he is about to say.

I tell you, Vivienne.
I disapprove.

VIVIENNE
Equally excited.

In defeating minor kings
He defeats their plant and animal spirits too,
Does he not?
He does injustice to their inner lives
While he blights their outer lives.

JOHN

He does defeat their spirits;
He thus offends the more
The dignity of all
Who treasure and deserve their dignity.
As a new and single social order rises,
So too a single faith.

A nation pieced together
Through falsely named "heroic" deeds:
Arthur with his weaponry.
A *Christian* nation then
Through falsely named "morality":
Arthur with his single Book.

VIVIENNE
Emotionally.

To dominate is not heroic;
Obedience is not morality.

JOHN

The domination of the many…
The many powerless human beings,
Their many cherished spirits,
The spirits of the earth and waters…
Overlooked.

VIVIENNE

Do we *look* at those
Who lose a footrace?
Many more who run
Will lose than win.

JOHN

Concentrating power
In one man, in one god,
Single winners both,
Thrusts the many who have lost
Into swamplands
Where they disappear from view.

VIVIENNE

You will bring them back.

JOHN

Our Arthur will want to run, to win – at first –
Just as Malory and the others have it.
But run and win because of youth
And misdirected ardor.
Twelve battles won,
His story as it stands.
Should not then a revelation
As he grows in wisdom turn him?
The battles must come undone.
Twelve done, twelve undone:
A mythic number.
From unjust glory for a victor
To justice for the many.

VIVIENNE

At last restoring dignity
To every person, however born.

JOHN

There is no dignity in obedience
To a distant master,
Neither to a living human master
Nor to a perfect and eternal one.
Obedience belongs to those we know and love,
Not to strangers or their agents or their laws.

VIVIENNE

A restoration like no other, John.

JOHN

Its time must come.

VIVIENNE

Contemplatively.

Dignity restored…
And dignity lives in the depths of the soul.
Your new music
Can reach those depths.

JOHN

The form for this substance
Simultaneous speech and sign.
Two different texts to make
A poetry never before experienced
Between the texts,
A counterpoint that draws
The soul's full content to light.

VIVIENNE
As if an announcement, beaming.

"Arthur Pendragon,"
A Play in Five Acts,
By John Keats.

John and Tom sit at the
table. John takes up
a sheet of paper. They
look up at Vivienne,
exultant.

JOHN and TOM
In unison, slowly.

I'll begin, I think,
In medias res…

Curtain

Equifinality

Cast of Characters

Fred, *an assistant professor of philosophy*

Julie, *an assistant professor of anthropology*

Harry, *a professor of physics*

Scenes

Scene 1

Fred's living room, a college town. At rise, Fred, in his early thirties and a recently hired faculty member at the college, paces. Julie, his contemporary and a member of the college's anthropology department, sits, watching him.

JULIE

I don't know what you mean, Fred. Why second best?

FRED

Once when I was an undergraduate in Chicago, Ernst Schleimann was invited to the university. He…

JULIE
Interrupting.

The pianist?

FRED

The same. All he had to do was live in one of the prairie houses for a term and talk to us informally. Four-o'clock teas a couple of times a week.

JULIE

No concerts?

FRED

There was one, a kind of gala. I didn't go.

JULIE

I wish I'd been there.

FRED

You would have enjoyed meeting him. I made a pest of myself talking to him at the teas. Toward the end of his residency he asked me what I was planning to do with myself. That's when the first-best and second-best vocations came up. He told me never to try to make a living doing what I loved best. I would corrupt it, or the world would corrupt it. Keep that activity locked away safe, he said, and do what you like second-best to make your place in the economy.

JULIE

I see that. It upsets me, though. I think I always wanted to be an anthropologist, and now I am one.

FRED
Joking.

Oh no, you've corrupted your work, or the world has corrupted it, or something else ironic has reared its ugly head.

JULIE
Seriously.

Don't joke. What if I *have* compromised? Ironies don't announce themselves to their victims. I may have compromised and not realized it.

FRED

Take it easy, Julie. You're the most careful person I know. You question everything.

JULIE

Skeptics miss less than other people, I guess.

FRED

Yes they do. Much less.

JULIE

Reflecting on her life.

I wasn't always…

Enthusiastically.

Wait. Aha. I *am* doing what I love second best. There were these alleys behind the apartment buildings in the neighborhood I grew up in. We weren't supposed to play in them, but I did anyway. One summer – I was eight or nine – I was playing alone behind our building and I saw an old lady shuffling down the alley carrying two shopping bags stuffed full. Cats erupted from behind garbage cans, meowing, their tails up. It was kibble she was carrying; she was feeding the cats. What a perfect life, I thought. No worries, helping creatures that unknowingly help us. I'd never admired anyone so much. That's what I wanted to do. *That* was my first best thing.

FRED
Cheerfully.

You have something to look forward to. After you've lived the anthropological life in exotic places, you can take a deep breath, shelve your accumulated plaudits, and live your first-best life as a bag lady. You'd hardly be doing that for money – unless there's something I don't know about cats – so you'd be entirely exempt from corruption.

JULIE

The arc of my life, clear at last. I'll be glad to shelve those plaudits eventually, to tell the truth; acquiring them is hard work and both the people I study and I myself disapprove of hard work. But speaking of the arcs of lives, is teaching philosophy to sleepy adolescents your first or second noblest aspiration?

FRED

I was a devoted English major before I had that conversation with Schleimann. I switched to philosophy afterward.

JULIE

I see. What you most wanted to do was write the Great American Novel. You didn't want to corrupt the process, so you surveyed the groves of academe anew and fixed on Plato and the boys. Confronting the big-time thinkers of the West for a living seemed like a reasonable if not ecstatic way to spend your time.

FRED

Precisely. You must have been there.

JULIE

I was in spirit.

FRED

I don't know why people like me need to aspire to that novel, but we do. Why compete with *Moby-Dick*?

JULIE

Do you think about the novel much?

FRED

I do. Walking to class, sometimes before going to sleep. Odd times.

JULIE

My first love in life doesn't take much thinking about. When the time comes, I'll simply fill up my shopping bags. You, on the other hand, have a big, longtime project, fraught with unknowns.

FRED

It's sustaining, though, in spite of the unknowns. The novel is a keel, in a way. Not unlike your picture of yourself happily calling out your alley-cat pals.

JULIE

There's a lot of duality in things, isn't there? Your outward life as a teacher and inner life piecing together a fictional world. My doing fieldwork in the Caribbean and peacefully wandering Cleveland's alleys.

FRED

I remember something in Gandhi's papers. You might live in a crowded, heartless city, but you needed to imagine yourself in a small, self-sufficient village so that what you did in the city would serve what you were imagining rather than what you were experiencing. His duality gave him a practical moral order. A person would always know what to do.

JULIE
As if lifting a wine glass.

Here's to double lives.

FRED
Following suit.

To double lives.

JULIE

Any of that in your novel – so far, I mean?

FRED

Novels live on characters not being what they appear to be – appearance/reality, say one thing/mean another. Think of the comedies that depend on mistaken identity. I mention that because what I most want to do is write a comic novel. Of tragedy there's enough in real life – too much.

JULIE

What's better than helping people smile? I applaud your aim.

FRED

Thanks. I need all the encouragement I can get.

JULIE

In the meantime, your philosophy…

FRED

That's why I thought we could have dinner with Harry tonight.

JULIE

Harry's a neat guy. I heard his cello recital last year. Not bad for the senior member of the physics department.

FRED

I went to his talk about the nature of time for physicists and the nature of time for musicians on Monday. I was impressed. He made the problem of time a pressing human question.

JULIE

I missed that talk. Rats. I'm preoccupied with the problem of time myself. The way time works in traditional societies like the ones I study is a huge issue. A whole passel of issues.

FRED

That's great. You have to tell me. I feel bad for exploiting you and Fred, but I've got to get a book out before tenure looms, and I was hoping to deal with time from a couple of perspectives. I've had an inkling for a while that anthropology and physics would help me out.

JULIE

We're here to help. A double perspective…

FRED

…yielding a monograph and job security.

JULIE

I'll mention an anthropological conundrum before Harry arrives. A friend of mine works in the Pacific. The people he studies look forward, so to speak – toward the past, not the future. They acknowledge no future. And more than that – as if that's not enough – it's not the past of dates and historical events they look forward at. It's a past that short-circuits history, short-circuits what we think the past *is,* and zips straight to an origin story that's outside of time. That story has so much energy and meaning for them that pulling it up fills their present from one moment to the next. So…there goes time under the aspect of clocks and calendars.

FRED
Excited.

That's a lot to assimilate at one hearing.

JULIE

It is.

FRED

They have no conception of the future? Really?

JULIE

None. Nor do they seem to be afraid of death. My death happens in the future, and I'm utterly convinced that there *is* a future, so my dying is a big deal to me. *The* big deal. Not so for these Pacific Islanders. The absence of that anxiety spreads to a general absence of anxiety. That's pretty good.

FRED

You're not kidding. The guys we philosophy teachers begin with tell us that philosophy itself begins at the point human beings become conscious of death. Maybe "afraid of death" is more accurate.

JULIE

The islanders traded philosophy for a cheerful presentism. Not a bad bargain.

FRED

Pacing more rapidly; as if to himself, heatedly.

And what about the denial of history? That practically denies *causality*, an event at time-one causing an event at time-one-plus-one. There *are* no times-one and one-plus-one. It denies *explanation,* a general law applying to all historical time, therefore applying to a specific event so that a later event is entailed. There go general laws and entailments. It denies *teleology,* one event being the means to the end of a later event. Causality, logical explanation, teleological explanation, all gone – everything we *teach!*

JULIE
Amused.

I must say that I wish my students, even my colleagues, got as wrought up over an anthropological observation as you do.

FRED

Your friend has pulled the rug out from under modernity.

JULIE

You're right. He has.

FRED
More calmly.

My book is going to need quite a long chapter before what I'd been thinking would be chapter one.

JULIE

It'll be a stronger book for it. I'll get you in touch with Michael. He'll be pleased to tell you all about his island. He loves it there more the longer he stays. His department worries that he'll go native.

FRED

Thanks, Julie. If ever I can return the favor…?

JULIE

Sometime you'll have to tell me what Immanuel Kant meant by the "noumenon." I never got it.

FRED

You're on.

                                        A knock at the door.

And here's Harry.

Scene 2

A restaurant. Julie, Fred, and Harry sit at a small table, coffee cups and wine glasses before them.

HARRY

I first thought there was something fishy about time when my ninth-grade teacher told us kids that an electron doesn't start out at the light-switch when we turn on the switch and then travels along the wire to the bulb. You flip the switch and Bang, all the electrons along the whole length of the wire are sizzling simultaneously. No traveling; no electron here one second and there a second later.

FRED
Excited.

No traveling…that sounds uncannily like a passage in a great book by Maurice Merleau-Ponty. He says that we're all in the habit of thinking of time as a river: water traveling *from* the mountains *to* where you're standing and then *on* to the sea; time "traveling" from the past toward the present, where you're standing, and then going toward the future. But in fact the snow melting high in the mountains, the river flowing in front of you, the river pouring into the sea: that's all happening at the same time; they're not successive states. It's like your wire, simultaneous sizzle. Then he says a wonderful thing, that the objective world is too much of a plenum for there to *be* time.

HARRY

No time along the wire, no time along the river…

JULIE

…and no time on Michael's island.

FRED

Merleau-Ponty talks about the "thick present"…

JULIE

…which sounds like the present of traditional peoples – and perhaps of all of us before the high civilizations gave us clock- and calendar-time and arrangement-making time…

FRED

…the kinds of time that must be thinning out the plenum and emptying the present.

HARRY

There's another way to get a plenum. You start out by denying that time exists. Instead of ending with that, you postulate it and see what happens. The first thing that happens is that you're stuck with a static universe. No time: no change, no motion.

FRED

Plato's universe is like that, static. What's real for him he calls "being," and being is as static as it comes. Plato despises the opposite of being, "becoming," which is all about movement and change.

HARRY

The physicists who argue the absence of time in the universe are strongly influenced by Plato, Fred. One of their lines of work posits a universe made up of an infinite number of "stills" – like the still-frames of a 35-millimeter movie. Movie film is made up of still-frames-in-a-row, every still a static snapshot. It's our persistence-of-vision that gives us the illusion of motion and the passing of time. An illusion. What we mistakenly believe to be objective time derives from a feature of our eyes and brains. Time isn't in the universe out there, ready-made.

JULIE

Whoa, speaking of counter-intuitive theories. I'm convinced every second that I'm experiencing real motion and time, features of the objective universe whether my eyes and brain are in the universe or not. Time seems fundamental to me. Evolution happens in time. But I have to give it to those colleagues of yours – an infinite number of stills is sure a plenum.

FRED

And we have a philosopher, Merleau-Ponty, saying there's no time in a plenum, and physicists, some of them anyway, saying essentially the same thing.

JULIE

You can add the thick present of traditional peoples. Their mental processes give them a moment-to-moment plenum, and the time they experience is so unlike clock- and calendar-time you can say there *is* no time for them.

FRED

Quite a convergence, I must say.

To Harry.

Like Julie, though, I don't see how you derive the world you and I live in from an infinite number of still-frames. In a can of movie film, the stills are fixed in celluloid, each one slightly different from the last. Simple. Reality is complicated.

HARRY

The stills that make up the universe are attached to each other like the stills in the can – not in celluloid, but according to a principle like "each one slightly different from the last," just as you say. Each still is very rich in detail – *very* complicated. Each one has a sort of formula associated with it that says, "attach me to *that* still over there, not to that other one." Their attachments make what one of us calls a "path" in the plenum of stills, which our brains read as motion and time just as our persistence-of-vision reads projected movie-stills as motion and time.

JULIE

So our brains create time out of timelessness?

FRED

You wanted to know what Kant meant by the noumenon, Julie. Part of what he meant is just what Harry has been talking about. Time is inside us. Outside? Who knows? Kant didn't say that the outside world was timeless, only that it was unknowable. What we see and hear and touch is an amalgam of that unknowable outside and our limited human equipment for knowing anything at all, our brains and senses.

HARRY

The plenum-of-frames theory is a complete story about the "outside," *pace* Kant – knowable in the classic modern way, via higher mathematics. But the theory does share a dependence on our accidental equipment for experiencing the world, just as Kant said.

JULIE

You can cut a frame or a group of frames out of a reel of movie film. You can rearrange frames. Is that possible in your theory, Harry?

HARRY

Cutting out a group of frames isn't a mere possibility; it's is a very common experience. It's what happens in dreams. A sequence of frames that would be uninterruptedly lengthy and commonsensical in the daytime can be truncated, rearranged this way or that way, as an episode or a tableau in a dream.

FRED

The formula for affiliating one frame with a particular next frame is non-negotiable in the daytime but negotiable at night? Is that what you're saying?

HARRY

Yup.

FRED
Trance-like.

So the universe is made of detached frames and clumps of frames. Dreams are made of detached frames and clumps of frames. The universe is a *dream*. Our waking lives are the exception, intervals of structure in a largely unstructured universe, an unimaginably… vast… dream. We're in the universe more intimately in the night than we are in the day.

JULIE

There's a novelistic notion for you, Fred.

HARRY

Or the occasion for an epic poem. "The Universe a Dream."

FRED
Normally.

I think I've heard that there's a great Spanish play called "Life is a Dream."

JULIE

It looks like nighttime life is a dream in a profounder way than we imagined.

FRED

It's James Joyce's night, the night of *Finnegans Wake…*

HARRY

…where syllables are like movie stills, and Joyce rearranges them to make new realities and new names for them.

JULIE

Here's one: can you rearrange the stills making up the universe – in the daytime? Can you *alter* those formulas that affiliate stills into the commonsense reality we all cleave to?

HARRY

My colleagues say no.

FRED

And you?

HARRY

I say possibly.

JULIE

Really?

HARRY

You said that the plenum of stills is counter-intuitive. Why not go a step farther in that direction?

FRED

But it doesn't happen.

HARRY

An infinite number of frames, Fred. And who knows how many copies of frames and clumps of frames, as you call them?

Scene 3

The college faculty club. Fred has just given a reading from his latest novel. He and Julie stand drinks in hand.

JULIE

I must tell you that I've attended a number of readings, august occasions all, but I've never heard the laughter that accompanied your chapter about Douglas and the gorilla.

FRED

That laughter is what I live for.

JULIE

Have you always wanted to be a novelist – the kind of novelist you are?

FRED

Yes, in fact.

JULIE

What benevolence, bringing laughter to so gloomy a world. I do anthropology here. No laughs.

FRED

Do you like doing anthropology?

JULIE

I do. Well, actually, it's the people I've met in the field I like – love. Primal people. They understand life, work very little, and laugh a lot. They're disappearing. I try to celebrate them.

FRED

That sounds like benevolence to me.

JULIE

Thanks. I need all the encouragement I can get.

FRED

It's interesting that you say that. I came close to shelving my literary ambitions when I was an undergraduate in Chicago. I remember…Ernst Schleimann was invited to the university for a year. He…

JULIE
Interrupting.

The pianist?

FRED

The same. All he had to do was live in one of the school's prairie houses for a term and talk to us informally. Four-o'clock teas a couple of times a week.

JULIE

No concerts?

FRED

There was one, a kind of gala. I didn't go.

JULIE

I wish I'd been there.

FRED

You would have been troubled talking to him, I think.

JULIE

Why?

FRED

I made a pest of myself talking to him at the teas. Toward the end of his residency he asked me what I was planning to do with myself. I'd been an English major and I had dreams of writing comic fiction. He told me never to try to make a living doing what I loved best. I would corrupt it, or the world would corrupt it. Keep that activity locked away safe, he said, and do what you love second-best to make a place in the economy.

JULIE

Interesting advice. You didn't take it.

FRED

I came close to taking it. I was a kid and Schleimann was a great man. He took an interest in me. I switched to the philosophy department the year after our conversations.

JULIE

You didn't care for philosophy finally?

FRED

On the contrary, I liked it very much. But I came to realize that Schleimann had applied a formula to me; he couldn't have known who I really was. His advice seemed like *noblesse oblige*. What you said, about needing encouragement? That's what I needed, not the advice of someone who was used to being listened to.

JULIE

Well, I, for one, am glad you went back to writing comic fiction.

FRED

It's kind of a truism that the novel began in comedy – you know, *Don Quixote*…

JULIE

I'm not a specialist, but I think *Don Quixote* is a terribly sad book.

FRED
Enthusiastically.

I couldn't agree more. I took wonderful Rabelais for inspiration instead. Not his plot or characters, but his language. The joy in his work is in the fullness and energy of his words. Laughter comes from his extravagance, his overflow of fullness. That produces a unique kind of laughter, different from how we modern guys respond to jokes. It's what I try to elicit.

JULIE
Excited.

You won't believe this, but the primal people I mentioned, whom I love so much, who laugh absolutely all the time, do so because of *their* fullness. I think we're onto the same thing.

FRED
Responding in kind.

Tell me about their…what…

JULIE

…thick time? It's the plenum they live in from one moment to the next. A friend of mine works in the Pacific. The people he studies look forward…toward the past, not the future. They acknowledge no future. And more than that – as if that's not enough – it's not the past of dates and historical events they look forward at, it's a past that short-circuits history, short-circuits what we think the past *is,* and goes straight to an origin story that's outside of time. That story has so much energy and meaning for them that pulling it up fills their present, moment to moment. So…there goes time under the aspect of clocks and calendars.

FRED
Excited.

That's a lot to assimilate at one hearing.

JULIE

Isn't it?

FRED

They have no conception of the future, you said?

JULIE

None. Nor do they seem to be afraid of death. My death happens in the future, and I'm utterly convinced that there *is* a future, so my dying is a big deal to me. *The* big deal. Not so for these Pacific Islanders. The absence of that anxiety spreads to a general absence of anxiety. That's pretty good.

FRED

You're not kidding. And you're right, we *are* onto the same thing.

JULIE

The connection between fullness somehow defined and laughter; the connection between emptiness and gloom…

FRED

I'm thinking that fullness achieved through language or through the astonishing kind of time your Pacific Islanders live in – that fullness implies a kind of moral order, too. Not hurting others, where people whose language is empty and whose time is thin are more likely to act out, *to* hurt others…

JULIE

...because they know that something has been stolen from them, but they don't know what.

> Harry enters

HARRY

Hi, Julie.

To Fred.

Mister Moreno, I wanted to tell you how much I enjoyed your reading. If I may say so, it was therapeutic. It's hard to hold onto the day's complaints while laughing so hard.

FRED

Thanks.

JULIE

Mister Moreno...

FRED

...Fred.

JULIE

Fred, this is Harry Turner, Professor of Music and cellist extraordinaire.

FRED

I'm certain that I would find your music-making as therapeutic as you found my prose.

HARRY

That would please me very much.

FRED

Julie and I have been talking about two approaches, or a double approach, to an idea of plenitude. One approach, from language – Lewis Carroll's "portmanteau words," Rabelais's incredible French, James Joyce's multiple-meanings. And a second approach, from a radically different species of temporality, such that time the way we live it doesn't exist and the present moment is far more full than any present moment modern urban types are capable of.

HARRY

I see.

Ruminating.

You remind me of Bach's Two-Part Inventions. Yes, a melody in the right hand, a melody in the left, and an unalterable conviction that something immense is going on. Time itself is being doubly lyricized by Bach. My teacher in Salzburg believed that the Inventions recapitulate the origin of the universe. There must be something profound indeed to doubling.

JULIE

Music thickening the present…

FRED
To Julie.

Exactly. I don't think that great music eliminates time, though, the way your Pacific people do. Bach seems to me to take everyday time, which is usually thin and cacophonic, and makes it thick and lyrical, the way Harry says. I think Bach *rescues* rather than eliminates time.

HARRY

Mozart wrote two Duos for Violin and Viola. He wrote them as a favor to Haydn's brother, who had a commission for six duos and could only finish four. So Mozart turned out two of the most wonderful pieces of music ever written practically overnight. There you have two again – making more music with two instruments than has been made for full orchestras from the death of Brahms to today.

JULIE
Lifting her glass.

Here's to duos

Scene 4

The college faculty club. Julie and Harry have just finished their cello/piano recital. Fred stands alone, drink in hand. After a moment, Julie and Harry enter.

FRED

Congratulations! What a wonderful recital.

JULIE

It wasn't us, it was Beethoven. The Opus 69 is the supreme cello sonata.

HARRY

Not even Brahms fully understood what a cello and piano can mean to each other.

JULIE

Or Beethoven afterward. The Opus 69 stands alone.

HARRY
To Julie.

I can't believe that you began the piano as an adult and you've come this far so quickly.

JULIE

Thanks, Harry. Don't underestimate your influence. I barely understood what phrasing was until we began to play together.

FRED
To Harry.

You ran into Schleimann in Salzburg, you said. It was a concert of his that started Julie out. In Chicago.

HARRY
To Julie.

Not Cleveland? I thought you and Fred came here from Cleveland.

JULIE

I was born there, but when I was in my late teens I went to Chicago on a whim. I was cleaning houses in Hyde Park when I met Fred.

FRED

I was at the University locked in battle with the Great Books.

JULIE

Come on. You loved those books.

FRED
To Harry.

I guess I did, but they were driving me crazy. To relax I'd take late-night walks around the neighborhood. One night I spied Julie in a woebegone alley, feeding the cats. She was quite a sight.

JULIE

Are you questioning my mastery of fashion?

FRED

I wouldn't dream of it. Wearing three sweaters, two or three skirts, a fedora, and two pairs of gloves missing their fingers was coming into vogue that season. You were in the vanguard.

JULIE

As always.

HARRY

And you weren't studying the piano at the time?

JULIE

You wouldn't believe what a slacker I was, Harry. I roamed Cleveland's alleys, then Chicago's alleys, taking whatever odd jobs would keep me in spaghetti. I was doing exactly what I wanted to do.

HARRY

I admire that.

FRED

Then the Schleimann concert. He was invited to the university for a year. All he had to do was live in one of the university's prairie houses and talk to us informally. Four-o'clock teas a couple of times a week. I made a pest of myself talking to him at the teas. He told me never to try to make a living doing what I loved best; I would corrupt it, or the world would corrupt it. Do what you like second-best to make a place in the economy, he said. Best advice I ever got. At the end of the term there was a kind of gala. Schleimann played a Bach/Beethoven concert. A set of Two Part Inventions and the last two Beethoven Sonatas.

JULIE

I insisted on going. It might have been a premonition; I don't know. I'd never felt part of the university gang, but I had to hear him.

HARRY

I understand perfectly. Schleimann radiated music. We followed him around in Salzburg. He would stop now and then and produce an epigram – in the spirit of *noblesse oblige,* I'm afraid, but the epigrams were jewels.

FRED
To Harry.

Julie was no slacker from then on, I must say. While I was trying to figure out Saint Bonaventura, Julie practiced. Did she *practice*.

JULIE

I never compromised my slacker code. "Only do what's fun, and never miss a night feeding the kitties." Practicing was fun – deep fun. I loved it. And I never missed a night.

FRED

We stayed in Chicago while I finished a Ph.D. in philosophy and Julie studied with Rona Bilstein.

JULIE

And then Fred got his job here…

HARRY

…and I heard you play Bach in the Student Union and begged you to play sonatas with me. Are you both happy here?

JULIE

I couldn't be happier.

FRED

Nor I. Of course I've got to get tenure so we can *stay* happy.

JULIE

Fred wants to write a book. I want him to write about music.

FRED

Maybe I can join philosophy up with music. It *should* be a good pairing, but I don't see it yet. My person is Kant, but Kant didn't have any feeling for music.

HARRY

I can help you there, Fred. You can approach music from Kant's great disciple Schopenhauer. He had a profound feeling for music. Schopenhauer argued that music brought us closer to reality than any of the arts or sciences, closer even than philosophy.

JULIE

What could "closer to reality" possibly mean?

FRED

Schopenhauer isn't much studied in graduate departments; why that is, I don't know. I haven't read him myself. I recall from histories of philosophy that he ran with Kant's conception of the noumenon. Noumenal reality was true reality for both Kant and Schopenhauer. Commonsense reality was of "phenomena," the results of human processing activity on noumenal things. Schopenhauer said something like, between things-in-themselves – his and Kant's noumenal things – and what we naively believe reality to be, stands the human brain.

JULIE

So music gets us closer to the noumenon?

HARRY

Yes. And you put "noumenon" correctly, in the singular. Kant posited a noumenal thing for every phenomenal thing. Schopenhauer posited one noumenon instead, a single, unknowable realm.

FRED

I like it, Harry. I'll read Schopenhauer.

JULIE

And you said that the brain stood between the noumenon and phenomenal reality, Fred. The brain. Schopenhauer wrote a long time ago, I assume. They probably didn't know much about the brain then. Now we talk about nothing else. Those fMRI's, all the flap about mirror neurons. It's front-page stuff. You could come at music from two directions, Schopenhauer back then and brain physics right now. You could read up on that, too.

HARRY

Doesn't philosophy abut on physics anyway, Fred?

FRED

Some philosophers think that if you ally modern logic with modern physics, you more-or-less get modern philosophy, yes.

HARRY

You could use physics in several ways, I think. The physics involved in the generation of music by string, brass, and woodwind instruments. The physics of its reception in the ear and the central nervous system. I don't think Schleimann would approve, but bringing Schopenhauer up to date as Julie suggests sounds like a legitimate project to me.

FRED

A binocular view of music, Schopenhauer and neuroscience.

JULIE

Tenure, an apartment with an extra bedroom.

HARRY

An ongoing series of cello/piano recitals, from Vivaldi to Shostakovich.

Scene 5

The restaurant. Julie, Fred, and Harry are in the positions they occupied at the end of Scene 2.

HARRY

I'm afraid that an infinite number of frames implies multiple universes, and we're now out of the intuition ballpark altogether.

JULIE

You don't mean to say that the three of us may be talking this way, or some other way, in a parallel universe right now.

HARRY

I do indeed mean that.

FRED

I can't tell you how much that cheers me up.

JULIE
Laughing.

Why in the world would that cheer you up?

FRED

You know how some people look up at a clear night sky and are either unmoved or discomfited by it? Other people, feeling just as small as the oblivious or uncomfortable ones who look up, are mysteriously *relieved.* The cosmic vastness gives their worries a new context. The galaxies make them feel lighter. So...the possibility that the three of us are conducting ourselves differently in parallel universes this very moment makes me feel that way – not because of something like the night sky but because of the multiplicity of simultaneous dramas. This particular drama now has a new context: there are other dramas, not necessarily proceeding like this one. So I feel lighter. Life leans in the direction of a dream instead of a problem.

JULIE

This drama, as you call it, is still the only one you've got. You have no access to the others.

FRED

I have no access to the uncountable number of planets other than Earth either. But because life on many of them may be going on more satisfactorily than it is on this planet, I feel consoled.

JULIE

Life isn't being conducted satisfactorily here?

HARRY

I must go with Fred on this one. Animals eat animals. I've never approved of that.

FRED

And look at what we humans have done to each other and to the Earth.

JULIE

I can see inferring other dispositions of life, or something like life, on other planets, and I can see feeling relief at looking up at the Milky Way, but what can anyone say about a conversation like this one going on right now in different ways in different universes? What, if anything, is constant in all or some of those conversations? Is anything duplicated? If yes, what, and why those things and not others? Are the upshots of the conversations different? Do the lives of which the conversations are episodes proceed in the same way? Do we all – the various Julies, I mean – end up in the same place? If not, where did various ones of us diverge? Doesn't all of that give you a headache?

FRED

No. I don't understand quantum gravity and that doesn't make my head hurt.

JULIE

Okay. We all have different degrees of toleration for unknowables.

HARRY
To Fred.

So you're alright with an infinite number of frames, and you're alright with time in Julie's neolithic places…

FRED

…and I'm intrigued with Kant's and Merleau-Ponty's relationships to your static universe, Harry, and to Julie's Pacific island. I think that I have the lineaments of a book now. I'll call it *Timelessness.*

JULIE
Wryly.

And your happiness with parallel worlds takes the pressure off working on it. It's not a problem.

FRED

Exactly. It's play. After all, another Fred might be playing at something else.

HARRY

Just as another I may be somewhat more the cellist than the physicist…

JULIE

…and another I?

FRED

Confess, Julie. Would you rather be feeding your alley-cats or preparing for the faculty meeting Friday night?

Nora Klein and World Peace

Chapter One

In Which I Introduce Myself

Humans actually think the wires connecting all these telephone poles are about telephones. Amazing, isn't it? My friend Alan told me his father is convinced that we live in a place called Chicago and this is 1946. Adults will believe anything. We orangutans are aware of how easily adults are fooled. The so-called wires are obviously the vines connecting all the trees in our green and mysterious forest. I'll explain.

Obviously I can get from one place to another really fast when I'm Beatrice or Romola, since Beatrice is a crow and Romola is a Canada goose. But sometimes I need to move like the wind *and* be especially strong, stronger than a crow or a Canada goose. So my arms aren't also wings right now; at this particular moment they're a lot longer and more powerful than my human-being arms. When I swing from vine to vine far above the forest floor, I practically fly. That surprises some people, because I'm otherwise slow-moving and dreamy, just like my fellow orangutans. When justice needs to be done, however, both strength and speed count.

This is my plan. The next time that bully George scares Alan after school, I'll take to the vines from wherever I am. I'll get to the two of them in no time. I'll leap down, grab George, swing back up, and hold onto him until he says he's sorry. Don't worry, I won't hurt him.

You'll have to pardon me for a minute. Silky just got out of his house again and I have to find him before a car does. Silky is Mrs. Greenberg's dog.

Look at all those cars! From above them, where I am, you would think that cars are the real people who live in Chicago and human beings are their slaves or something. But I forgot; the so-called cars are tigers with blood dripping from their fangs. That one went right through a red light. I'd lift it up to my vine the way I'd lift George, but I'm not *that* strong.

Silky is quite stupid. We all love him, but he's stupid. He doesn't believe cars exist. I wonder if he looks through them instead of at them. Do you suppose he sees what's on their other side, as if they weren't there? Even if he does, it wouldn't be worth it, because they *are* there, and they eat stupid dogs.

I haven't been to this particular neighborhood before. The signs on the store windows are all in two languages. That's what I call a good idea. The people who've lived here a long time can read the English, and the people who just got here from another country can read the other language, theirs. In our neighborhood all the signs are in English. We live in the back of my pop's store. The stitcher and the finishing machine are in the front of the store and we live behind the wall pop put up half way back. He fixes shoes.

There's Silky. All he ever wants to do is play around. He never watches where he's going. I have to be careful not to scare him when I drop down from up here. That would be horrible, my scaring him into the street in front of a car. Okay...okay. I've *got* you, you bum, and no amount of licking is going to change my mind. We're going back to your house. Mrs. Greenberg is probably having a fit worrying about you.

My grandfather, mom's father, lives with us. He plays the violin. If somebody asked me what makes me happiest, I'd say listening to him play late at night. I always go with him to the record store. He finds a record by Bach or Brahms, and then we go to the cafeteria and have black bread, baked beans, and coffee. My coffee is still mostly milk and sugar. I hope none of my friends ever notice that. I would be embarrassed. Going with him to the record store and then to the cafeteria is my second happiest time.

I mentioned Beatrice and Romola. The name mom and pop gave me twelve years ago is Nora. I have no objection to that. When I'm Beatrice...well, I'm myself and a crow, both at once. The same when I'm Romola the Canada goose. I'm currently working on being Omu the orangutan, *plus* Romola, *plus* myself, all three at the same time. I haven't decided whether that means being me and an orangutan with wings, say, so I'd still only be two people at once, or me and a separate hundred per cent orangutan and a separate hundred per cent Canada goose. I'll keep you informed.

Chapter Two

In Which Justice is Done to Mister Figgins

Many humans don't care for crows. What can I say? Crows are beautiful, they're smart, and they're fine alone and with other crows. People think crows make ugly noises when there are a lot of them together. It's people who make ugly noises.

One such person is Mister Figgins. He teaches the sixth- grade social-studies class Alan, George, and I were in last year. Being a sixth-grade teacher is already one strike against him. I don't mean to be unfair, but sixth grade was absolutely terrible. You got homework. No one should be associated with sixth grade.

For homework once, Mister Figgins told us to write about the war being over. We were still reading about the *Civil* War, so we had to find out about 1939 and 1941 and the end of the war on our own. I didn't have much trouble because mom had gone to the movies every Friday night for eight weeks and she brought home books about history and other subjects. They went on sale there on Fridays. I read the book that included the war over the weekend, then lent the book to Alan, and wrote my three pages for Monday. On Tuesday the disaster struck. Alan didn't write the essay Mister Figgins wanted.

"Alan," Mister Figgins said at the start of class, "what do you mean when you write, 'I don't think anybody should have died in the war?' Surely you mean any American boys. The enemy deserved to die." Alan turned purple. Anybody would have, but Alan is a *very* shy person. Teachers shouldn't make shy kids wish they could disappear. He couldn't talk. "Well, Alan? We're waiting," Mister Figgins said. George looked back at Alan and laughed. Finally Alan just barely got out, "Nobody deserves to die like that." You will not believe what our beloved teacher said next. He said he thought it would be a good idea to call up Alan's *father*.

I'm perched on the top branch of the danger tree with several of my cousin crows. Humans call the danger tree that because it leans over the school parking lot. They dislike the tree and positively hate such crows as myself who perch on it and poop on their cars. I'm waiting patiently. The breeze is quite nice. My branch is swaying just enough to be fun. Yes, that's the bell ringing. A few more minutes. I wonder if Mister Figgins will be wearing a hat. I truly hope not.

We crows are artists. We're not appreciated as we should be. Naturally I scored a direct hit to the top of Mister Figgins's head. That made me a competent crow, but not an artist. It was when Mister Figgins *looked up,* which he really should not have done, that I rose to the level of art. I splotched him a second time, right on his crumby face. *Nobody* makes my friend Alan cry.

While I'm at it, I'll ride the rising air toward the lake. I'm not moving one wing feather, and I'm going *up!* When I glide going down, I weigh nothing; when I glide going up, I weigh *less* than nothing. It's a lot like the feeling I have when I hear grandpa play the violin.

Chapter Three

Alan and I Go Downtown

My parents and Alan's father work night and day, so Alan and I have time to go anywhere we want to as long as we're careful, which we always are. One Saturday morning mom packed four hard-rolls in a bag and Alan's father gave us a dollar over streetcar fare. (Alan's mother was killed in the war. His father says Hitler killed her.)

We stayed in the neighborhood, for the movies. There are five movie theaters within walking distance of us. We went to the one that added three cartoons to the double feature at the first show. That theater looked like what we imagined an Egyptian palace would look like. Golden columns held up the high ceiling, which was dark blue speckled with stars. When the lights went out, the stars lit up. Nobody knew where we were, and the seats were soft, and there was a Humphrey Bogart movie and a Tarzan movie. We finished our rolls, which were perfect, crispy on the outside and super-soft on the inside, before the cartoons came on. We would have stayed to see the whole show over again, but we decided to go downtown instead.

The reason I like streetcars as much as I do is that the front looks exactly like the back. Sometimes I take the streetcar to the end of the line just so I can watch the conductor switch to the other end and start up in the opposite direction. My job would be to swing the backs of the streetcar's seats around. I ride to the end of the line especially in the summer. The end of the line opposite from downtown isn't like the city at all. The grass is as high as my knees in every direction and there's not a single building. I get off, and when the streetcar starts back, I walk into the grass and become a dragonfly. The sun shines through my wings and turns them colors. I don't fly far. I hover, standing still in the air. I catch the next streetcar home.

Alan and I got on the streetcar for downtown and stood up the whole way even though there were seats. We sat enough watching Humphrey Bogart and Johnny Weissmuller. Also, when you hold on, you rock with the streetcar. Both of us like to do that.

It was a straight line riding to the edge of downtown, and then you walked. The wind was blowing that Saturday, so walking was fun because we had to lean way forward. When the wind let up, we practically fell on our faces. On one side of you is the lakeside park, and on the other side one tall building after another. As the sun went down, the neon signs on top of our favorite buildings came on, and people inside the buildings turned on their lights. The buildings became like a sky full of stars or the ceiling of the Egyptian movie theater. The wind howled in our ears. We were courageous explorers who couldn't be stopped by a mere hurricane.

Our destination was a huge hotel with an arcade in it. Whoever thought up arcades was a genius. You can walk around looking in store windows; you're *inside* the hotel, but *outside* the arcade stores. If it's cold in the real outside, you're warm even though you're outside the stores. Also the light outside the stores is inside light, not outside light, sunlight. I mention that because looking in a store window when you're in the arcade, you see what's in the store, but you also see your own reflection. If the window were a regular window, outside, you would see what's in the store and maybe a dim reflection of yourself. In the arcade you see yourself as clearly as you see inside the store. That's amazing to me.

We went through the arcade's revolving door only one full turn because there was a crowd of people going in and out. Two or three turns are more dignified, but you can't have everything. Alan likes to look in the toystore window. There was usually a model steam engine in it, that worked. He loves that steam engine, and some day I'm going to get it for him, mark my words. We spent quite a lot of time at that window. Then we walked down the arcade to a window with men's hats displayed in it. I'm fascinated with those hats. There's a doberman pinscher inside the store. I wouldn't go inside for a hundred dollars, but I can't get enough of the hats in the window. There's a black derby right next to a fancy cowboy hat. I bet the British prime minister wears the cowboy hat and a cowboy wears the derby.

We were looking at ridiculous jewelry with little spotlights making it sparkle when Alan asked me a hard question. "If we made believe we were elephants, would we see elephants in the windowglass?" I had never thought of reflections that way. I said that there was only one way to know. I asked Alan if he could reach the apples high up in those apple trees with his trunk. He said that he definitely could, and that he especially enjoyed sucking water up his trunk and then spraying people. I liked to spray myself, after getting dirty on purpose so that I could have mud all over me. We both clump-clumped through the jungle, careful not to step on other animals. Monkeys were chattering all around us and shining orange and purple birds screeched on branches overhead. "I sort of *see* us," Alan whispered. "Me too," I said.

Chapter Four

That True Love May Prevail

I don't want to be a bother, but my extremely important school project required some bothering. You could say that the project began in the record store.

Grandpa and I were in the record store as usual. He had heard something on the radio by Bach and he wanted to buy a record of it. Mister Schwartz was telling grandpa about different violinists, so I riffled through bins looking at labels. Who should walk into the store but Mister Peterson. Mister Peterson is handsomer than Cary Grant and Jimmy Stewart put together. He is also nicer than Ronald Coleman in *Lost Horizon*. He teaches English.

"Hello, Nora. What a pleasure to see you." Mister Peterson is also very polite.

"Hello, Mister Peterson," I said. Not very original. I should have waited a second and said something smart.

"Are you looking for anything in particular?"

"My grandfather is. It's a piece by Johann Sebastian Bach for the violin by itself. My grandfather plays the violin."

"That's wonderful, Nora. Do you like Bach too?"

"I love Bach." That's more like it.

"That makes three of us. May I meet your grandfather?"

"Sure," I said.

I pulled grandpa over to us.

"This is Mister Peterson, grandpa," I said. "He's my English teacher."

Grandpa was very interested to know this. "You're Nora's teacher? She reads all the time. I help her pick books. Her parents also help her. She goes to the library and the librarian suggests books. She has an imagination to beat the band."

"There's nothing like reading on your own," Mister Peterson said. "Nora often writes as if she's someone else, just as famous writers do. I always look forward to her compositions."

I was standing right there. What an embarrassing thing to say. Grandpa couldn't get enough of it, though.

"At home she tells us what animals think."

That was too much. I interrupted grandpa. Who knows what he would have said next, and how Mister Peterson would have embarrassed me next.

"My grandfather knows everything about music, Mister Peterson. Maybe he can help you if you're trying to find an album."

Mister Peterson smiled. I think he knew that I changed the subject to get attention off me. He decided to be on my side. That's why I like him. He's on the kids' side all the time at school.

"In fact, I am looking for an album, the Beethoven Violin Concerto. Nora tells me that you play the violin. Do you have a favorite performance of the Beethoven?"

You ask a question like that, and grandpa immediately seems younger and straight instead of old and bent over.

"Do I have a favorite performance? You must understand the *stakes* here. Podolski or Grunbaum; the others, forget. Podolski is a perfect violinist. Machines are perfect, young man. Human beings *are* not and *should* not be perfect. Grunbaum is a violinist who thinks and feels, and he shows us how a violin thinks and feels – think-and-feel, one word. You're on one side or the other, do you understand? The future will belong to machines, or it will belong to human beings."

I'd heard this before, but every time grandpa starts on "there are two kinds of people," I get the shivers anyway. My mom and pop talk to each other about President Roosevelt and whether Stalin is a bad man or a good man. They're quite calm about President Roosevelt and Stalin. Grandpa talks to *me* about Podolski and Grunbaum, and he's absolutely not calm about them. He's an emotional person, and I suppose I am too. Mister Peterson got more than he bargained for when he asked about Beethoven. I was glad to see that he appreciated how seriously grandpa took his question.

"I can't thank you enough. The Grunbaum performance it is." He turned to me. "I can make my purchase now, and I'll be off. I'm certainly lucky that you and your grandfather were here."

Grandpa and Mister Peterson shook hands. I knew I had to do something big for Mister Peterson. My project was taking shape.

It's Tuesday after school. I'm soaring high over the neighborhood. When I'm with my fellow Canada geese, we fly together in our long lines, joining other lines, splitting off, settling on the lake, rising from the lake, together. We're one mighty bird, singing out our joy in flight. This afternoon, though, I'm alone, looking in on Mister Peterson.

He isn't walking toward his apartment building. Alan told me where his building is and that he lives alone. Alan delivers clothes for his father, who's a tailor, and Mister Peterson is one of his father's customers. Look at that. He's standing in front of the court building facing the park. *I* know who lives there. *Miss Vasquez* lives there. Alan says she tips him a quarter. Wait a minute, wait a *minute*. One, Mister Peterson lives alone. Two, Miss Vasquez lives alone. Three, Mister One stands starry-eyed in front of Miss Two's building. What am I to conclude from this, Doctor Watson?

Miss Vasquez always went outside at recess to make sure we didn't all kill each other. I'd gone over to talk to her before, about things like what the school would be doing about Valentine's Day. She's a really gentle person, a perfect third-grade teacher. I thought I'd casually bump into her.

"Hi, Miss Vasquez."

"Hi...Nora, isn't it?"

"Yup."

"How have you been, Nora? You were awfully good in 'The Man Who Came to Dinner' last month. I've been meaning to come to your English class to compliment you. You're a natural actress."

"Thank you. I guess acting does come naturally to me for some reason." Sure, she wanted to come to Mister Peterson's class to see *me*. It was all crystal clear now. "It's a funny play. By the way, I've been thinking about something, Miss Vasquez. You know Beethoven, the composer?"

"Of course I do, Nora. He's a wonderful composer."

"My grandfather is a terrific fan of Beethoven. He says that there are pieces by Beethoven that anybody, even children, can love. Like the Fifth Symphony? That was on the radio all the time during the war. I more-or-less remember that."

"Yes, it was on all the time. I agree with your grandfather. I can't imagine anyone not loving the Fifth Symphony."

"What I was thinking was, I bet third grade is a good time for people to get to know Beethoven. Music of his could be playing when kids are coming into the room. They'd hear it without even knowing that it was classical. They'd probably ask to hear more."

"Nora, what a tremendous idea!"

"My grandfather says that Mister Schwartz's record store has Fifth Symphony albums played by different orchestras. He'd let you hear them, I know. You could pick one. You could go tomorrow after school if you don't have something else to do."

"Actually, Nora, I haven't anything else to do, and I will go to Mister Schwartz's record store."

"Woops, recess is almost over. Bye, Miss Vasquez."

Next, to accidentally meet Mister Peterson after school.

"Oh, hello, Mister Peterson."

"Hello, Nora. Are you on your way home?"

"Yup. I liked what you read out loud today."

"*Great Expectations* is one of my favorite books."

"I'm glad I ran into you, Mister Peterson. I'm going to the record store by myself after school tomorrow. I want to talk to the record man about something, a surprise for my grandfather. You know him now; I thought you might like to help me. If you have a minute...?"

"Of course. I've been thinking about how I could return your grandfather's kindness. The performance of the Beethoven Concerto he recommended is now one of my treasures. Perhaps I can make a contribution to a gift."

"That would be great. I'll wait for you at the teachers' entrance."

Miss Vasquez stayed around to help George's little sister, so Mister Peterson and I arrived at the store before she did. What I said about a surprise for grandpa was absolutely true. I'd been saving from what pop gives me for chocolate bars so I could give him a record he didn't have. What Mister Peterson wanted to add made it a whole album, a complete Bach violin sonata instead of just one movement. Miss Vasquez came in just as Mister Schwartz

125

was wrapping up the album. First Miss Vasquez's face turned bright pink, then Mister Peterson began to stutter.

"M-m-miss Vasquez, h-how nice to see you."

"I'm so...how nice to see you, too. Nora, what a happy meeting."

Miss Vasquez definitely caught on. Mister Peterson had no idea what was happening. I ought to work for President Truman. I quietly slipped away with my package. A person can only do so much on a project, and then bow out.

Chapter Five

Alan

My life is easy, because I have my mom and pop and grandpa. It's different for Alan. His father is a fine person and he loves Alan, but he's sad most the time. He works in his tailor shop from morning until night, the way pop does. But Pop sings the whole time he puts soles and heels on people's shoes. Alan's father just works and works some more.

You might not think a tailor shop is a magic place, but it is. Alan wants to be with his father as much as he can, so sometimes he and I are in the shop from after supper to late at night. My parents know where I am; they can see the tailor sign from pop's bench. We get rid of our homework as soon as possible, like a couple of snakes shedding their skins. Then the four crowded racks of cleaned suits and dresses and coats in the back of the shop becomes our world of adventure.

First, we draw a circle on the floor. A tailor always has chalk. We put our entire collection of marbles, except the shooters naturally, inside the circle. The floor is old wooden planks, full of ups and downs. When one of us shoots a marble out of the circle, there's no telling where it will roll to. That's the beauty of it. We follow the marble on our knees, usually into the dark underneath of one of the clothes-racks. There might be a heavy overcoat almost touching the floor that's definitely a bear, or scarves on a hanger that are palm leaves on a tropical island. We try to shoot the wandering marble back into the circle, shuffling after it, crossing mountain ranges, bravely leaping over crevices, and dodging fierce leopards. Alan seems happy those times. He forgets about school, and especially about his mother, even though he never knew her.

Once we were in a pitch black corner looking for the marble. Alan's father only uses one light bulb in the shop, and that's in the front, over the sewing machine. There was a whole bank of overcoats in that corner, so we were on our stomachs feeling around for the escaped criminal. I remembered a particular page in one of the books about nature that mom brought home from the movies. People don't think about worms much, it said, and we don't think much *of* worms when we do think about them. In fact, though, worms are heroes. They burrow holes in the soil so air and water will run through it. Nothing would grow without more worm tunnels in the soil than you could possibly count. And if nothing grew, *we* wouldn't be around to think about worms or anything else.

I'm slowly slithering in the earth. It's always dark down here. Ha! I bumped into a root. I'll have to go around it. What's this? It's wet over here. That's fine with me, but I have to be careful. I don't want to *drown*, do I? D-d-d-drm, drm; vibrations, commotion above me. Animals. I don't think I'll go up to see what's on the surface today. I don't want to get *stepped* on, do I? It's too light up there, anyway. It makes me nervous to be seen. What if a *robin* sees me. I can't think about that. Oh no, another root...

Alan asked me what I was doing. I told him I was a worm. He *loved* that. He became a worm, too. He's a true sport. There are times, though, when playing in the back of the shop doesn't cheer Alan up. In the winter, on weekends, we have a special method for dealing with feeling really bad. We take the streetcar downtown, the way we do when we go to the arcade, but instead of walking parallel to the lake to the hotel, we go right up to the lake. You're not supposed to get too close to Lake Michigan; there are big boulders along the shore that keep you away. Nobody is there on freezing cold days, though, so we climb onto the boulders. When I think about it, it's a crazy thing to do, because the lake is choppy and the boulders are slippery and neither of us knows how to swim.

Once we're on a boulder we can sit on facing the lake, we begin to holler. What you have to know is how loud the surf and the wind are. Nobody could possibly hear us. If people saw our backs, they'd think we were just sitting there looking at the water. We do look at the water, but mainly what we do is scream. I never found it hard to scream, but I had to teach Alan how. He's very shy, as I said. But he got good at it eventually, and now he's better than I am. When our throats hurt too much to make another sound, we get up holding on to each other because of the slipperiness, and we get back onto the good old sidewalk. What we like to do before we go home is have a donut and coffee. We both know that coffee with our fathers has almost no coffee in it, but if we have the money on these special winter Saturdays, we have black coffee with our donuts. We choke a little, but the black coffee and our secret screaming make the time ours.

Chapter Six

War and Peace

"Mister Peterson, can I see you after school? It's about English."

"Of course, Nora. Why don't you come back to the room. I'll wait for you here."

Three o'clock came.

"Yes, Nora?"

"I've been thinking about the war. We wrote about it in Mister Figgins's class. I think about it for other reasons, too. Some people right in this neighborhood lost a family member in the war. That's so terrible, Mister Peterson. It's hard to imagine being okay after that."

"I agree with you, Nora. It's only luck if you haven't lost someone. We have to help those who weren't lucky in any way we can."

"Yes."

"Is there someone in particular?"

Secrets are secrets.

"No, it's not that. It's about English. I think about all the smart people who have written about ending wars. Not that I know who all of them are, but I do know it hasn't *worked,* Mister Peterson. People aren't getting smarter, I don't think. That means it'll *never* work."

"Don't think like that, Nora."

"But I do."

"One day there will be something no one has thought of, something that will stop the senseless and tragic killing of war."

"That's just it. Something no one has thought of. It's not like solving a math problem. We don't know how to do that if the problem is war. But somebody might just dream something up. Shouldn't we try absolutely everything?"

"We should."

"I've dreamt something up."

"What *is* it, Nora?"

See? Mister Peterson is on our side. He listens.

"Animals don't have wars. We have to be animals."

"But we're human beings. Oh, I understand. We're also animals, but with some added capacities, human capacities, like language. I confess, though; I don't know how we could be like animals and be human, too. I don't know what that would mean."

"Not be *like* animals, Mister Peterson, *be* animals and be human beings, at the same time."

"Goodness, Nora. I need a minute to think that through."

"Here's what I mean. Stuff written about ending wars hasn't worked. That might *not* be because those guys weren't smart. It might be because they weren't using the right language in the first place."

"Do you mean like using French instead of English? Many peace agreements have been written in French."

"No. I guess I don't mean another language. I mean another *kind* of language. You couldn't talk it, but you could write it. It would have an animal part and a human-being part in it at the same time. If a person is both a human being and an animal, a complete language would have two voices, not one, wouldn't it? Maybe we've been writing in *half* a language all this time."

"Here's paper and pencil, Nora. Show me."

"First write a few lines of human being. I'll do that. They'll be the (n), for Nora, lines.

I wish with all my heart

That there was no more war

And everybody would eat

And be warm in winter

And have good friends.

Next, I'll write lines that an animal, let's say an orangutan, might write. I need to write those lines, call them (o), for orangutan, lines, to match up a little with the (n) lines. This way:

> I play all the day, high
> Up in tall skinny trees.
> It's extremely hot up there.
> The birds are bright blue there.
> They are my friends.

Then you make pairs, because it's a person-plus-orangutan talking, and you want to hear both voices at once.

(n) I wish with all my   heart
(o) I play   all   the day, high

(n) That there was no more war
(o) Up   in   tall skinny trees.

(n) And everybody   would eat
(o) It's extremely hot   up   there.

(n) And be warm in   winter
(o) The birds are bright blue there.

(n) And have good friends.
(o) They are   my friends.

When people read this, they can read all the (n) lines first if they want to. They make sense by themselves. Then they can read the (o) lines. But the real and true reading comes next, reading each *pair* of lines as if it was a single line. So in the first pair, 'wish' and 'play' would get into your head at the same time, 'my' and 'day' at the same time, 'heart' and 'high' at the same time."

"It would be like playing the piano, wouldn't it, Nora? You're reading two lines at once when you're playing a piece on the piano, just as you're describing – but playing notes instead of words," Mister Peterson said.

"Yes, yes, yes. I like your word better, Mister Peterson; you *play* my lines, not read them. Play them, in your mind."

Mister Peterson was definitely sympathetic, but confused, too. "Why would someone decide to read and write this way? What was in your mind, Nora?"

That's a fair question. I said, "First, if a person is two somethings, and each something has a voice, it's only right that we hear both voices. If we had two *throats,* then we would hear both voices in the real outside world where *sounds* are. But we only have *one* throat, so we have to *write* the two voices and hear them in our *heads*. Maybe when you write like this, you *imagine* more and *think* more about what people really are. The animal part of a person doesn't make war; maybe that part can persuade the human-being part not to make war. It's as if right now we're only being half ourselves, and half-people are kind of crazy. Crazy people make wars even when they're smart. Whole people are sane. Sane people don't make wars."

"I want to go home and read what you've written slowly, and think about what you've said, Nora. You've done a fascinating and brave thing. I'll see you tomorrow."

Chapter Seven

In Which I Enter a Contest

It's not a simple thing to show somebody something as private as my new way to write. I kept waking up and going back to sleep and waking up again at night. I had to talk to Alan about this at lunch, before English class.

"I talked to Mister Peterson about the double-line stuff yesterday."

"Yay. It's about time."

"I wrote out the thing I showed you on Sunday."

"It only took me a minute to read it, Nora, I swear. I told you; it made me feel sort of warm. I never read anything that made me feel warm before. I had to take off my sweater."

"I really got a kick out of that. But you know? it won't be the same with grown-ups. They're set in their ways. I asked mom to read it and she said she couldn't make heads or tails of it. Mister Peterson was nice as could be, but he had to think about it, he said."

"That's better than nothing. A lot better. I don't know why people don't just jump in, though. It's fun to squinch your eyes and read two lines at once instead of one line at once. So what if it takes a little longer; it's fun."

"I'm with you, absolutely. You know what he said? It's like playing the piano. I think 'playing' is a better word than 'reading' for how you go from left to right taking in two lines at the same time. It's better to play than anything."

"I wish we played more at school."

"Shhh, Keemosaby. They'll come arrest you for saying something as horribly terrifying as that. We must not reveal that you are the Lone Ranger."

"Have a piece of cake, Tonto. My dad, I mean the Green Hornet, gave me two pieces."

English was great. Mister Peterson likes to read aloud from his favorite books. I love being read to. He read a story by P.G. Wodehouse that made us all laugh. Not so many books are funny, as far as I know. I think writers who make you laugh should have statues made of them. At the end of class, Mister Peterson asked me if I would like to have a chocolate sundae with him and Miss Vasquez at Anton's Ice Cream after school. Imagine that. Mister Peterson and Miss Vasquez.

They looked serious. It was a little strange to be ordering three chocolate sundaes looking that serious. Were they the last sundaes before the Martians came down inside balloons like Glinda in *The Wizard of Oz* to make everything different? I should have told them that Martians are nice people and sundaes are their main food.

"Miss Vasquez has a good idea, Nora."

Aha! One, Mister Peterson saw Miss Vasquez last night. Perfect. Two, he showed her my composition. Not so perfect. What if she thought I was crazy?

"Nora, I've never seen anything like your writing," she said. I was finished for good. I was Jimmy Cagney and that was my last meal before I got the chair.

"I was telling Mister Peterson about the *Daily Herald* contest. Do you know about that, Nora?"

"Nope."

"Well, the *Daily Herald* would like schoolchildren in Chicago to think about world peace now that the war has been over for a few months. Children from third grade to eighth grade can enter the contest. Mister Peterson and I would like you to enter. Would you like that?"

You show one person. Then that person shows somebody else. Then a million people know about you. Death from embarrassment is not pretty.

"I don't know, Miss Vasquez. I'll ask my mom. I'll tell you tomorrow."

"Take your time, Nora," Mister Peterson said. "We can understand that this is very personal for you. Do remember what you said, that we have to try everything? People will want to hear about something as new as what you've invented."

"Okay."

The sundae was good, anyway.

I haven't said very much about my mom. She isn't home too much. Grandpa is home all day. Of course pop is too, in a way, working in the front of the store. But I don't talk to pop a lot. He smokes cigars, sings, hammers and sews, and talks to buddies who come in. So I mainly talk to grandpa, grandpa and Alan. It's not mom's fault that she isn't home. We need a little more money than pop makes because he doesn't charge much for repairing shoes. Mom gets odd jobs around. She's the night cashier now at the movie theater where she bought the books she brought home for me. During the day she cleans people's apartments.

Mom always cooks breakfast and supper, though. She puts all kinds of vegetables and a huge bone with some meat on it in a pot in the morning for grandpa to watch during the day. I like those suppers. Grandpa was in front talking to pop about baseball or something, mom was stirring the pot, and I was ready to spring the contest on her.

"Mom? Mister Peterson and Miss Vasquez treated me to a chocolate sundae after school today."

Mom smiled in her truly beautiful way.

"Now let me take that in, honey. I'm not sure I know who Miss Vasquez is. It's also unusual for a teacher to take a student out for ice cream, isn't it?"

"Miss Vasquez teaches third grade at school. They're friends, Miss Vasquez and Mister Peterson. I showed them the funny writing that I do. They wanted to talk to me about it, and I guess they thought it would be nice to talk at Anton's."

"They liked your writing?"

"I guess they did. They want me to describe it in a newspaper contest. I told them I'd ask you first."

"Do you want to enter this contest?"

"I don't know, mom. People might think I'm nuts."

"No one will think you're nuts, Nora. You're the smartest and the best. Let them ask me, because I know."

She stopped stirring and we sat down at the table.

"Would you like some bread and butter before I call in your father and grandpa?"

"No thanks."

"Tell me what would happen if you won this contest. Would you be happy? Would something change that you wish would change? What."

"Some people might be a little kinder to other people. That's the change I'd want."

"And this might happen at the same time some other people thought that your writing is..."

"Stupid. They'd think it was stupid."

"Stupid it's not, but let's even say that some stupid people would think so. Would some people being kinder mean more to you than some other people thinking your writing was stupid?"

"Of course it would, mom."

"Then enter the contest, honey."

Chapter Eight

Alan's Song

There was too much going on.

I'm standing right here, taller than that house, my branches reaching up into the sky, my roots reaching down into the dirt. Well, a whole orchestra of crows is settling on my branches. Noble birds, crows. Black and handsome. Many notes and rhythms in their conversation. Aha, tickles: worms among my roots, as always. Now there you have heroic fellows. Charging ahead – if you call wiggling charging – without a care. I confess that I work quite hard, raising water through my trunk and branches to my lovely leaves, against gravity. The beauty of it is that my spread of leaves is just where it belongs in order to return water to the air. Out some of the water goes, round and round among all the other trees and plants and animals it floats, and down it comes again to the earth, keeping us all okay. Right now *I* am getting rained on, thanks to all my cousin trees.

Being me and a tree is a high-class rest from major commotion, I must say.

I spent a week writing my composition about double-writing for the newspaper. That's what I thought I'd call it, "double-writing." I put in three examples of it at the end of the composition. I hoped that the newspaper people would get warm when they played the examples, the way Alan had. Mister Peterson wanted to see what I'd written; Miss Vasquez, too. They meant well, without question. They couldn't be more considerate to me. But I wanted to write it and send it in to the newspaper by myself, without help. They would have made the composition better. But it wouldn't have been my composition.

I told Alan that I needed the week to put all of it together. He said he'd spend that week doing double-writing himself. He wanted to imagine a planet with no killing on it. He told me that his planet wouldn't even have animals, because animals eat animals. Plus he wanted to imagine the whole universe as if it were made of music, because he thought that was what my grandpa believed. Alan is absolutely right; grandpa believes that. Alan is crazy about grandpa. His double-writing would put his new planet on the first lines and his musical universe on the second lines, "to be read, I mean played, like on the piano, plunk, plunk, at the same time," Alan said, laughing in the way you laugh when you're a sweetie-pie and you're making fun of yourself.

He gave this to me the day I put my composition in the mailbox.

The trees are like swaying reeds.
 Silence, and   a   few sparkles

They're very   tall.
That   remain still.

Small white flowers grow
Then   very faint   sounds

From their stems and branches.
Can   be   heard, just barely.

The leaves make a thick green umbrella.
The   sparkling   lights begin to move

It's hot way up there.
Toward each other.

The ground is cool.
The sounds become

Ferns grow in   the shadows.
Like a gentle,   slow   music.

The high branches wind into each other.
The sparkling lights now   concentrated,

At   the top,
Shine brightly.

It's like there's only   one huge green tree.
The light and   music grow   together.

Nothing kills or   is killed   below it.
The music swells and swells, everywhere;

A   long time   ago,
And light is everywhere.

The umbrella   covered   the whole planet.
The music and   light flowed like a   river,

One tree-mind,
 An   ocean.

Telling   stories.
Songs and stars.

Alan said it made him feel good to write this way. I thought, Who *cares* about contests. Contests shmontests. It makes him feel good. That's enough for me.

Chapter Nine

In Which Losing is Winning

Waiting for the mailman is like being cursed. You can't start thinking about the day until you look at the mail. Then you look at the mail, and what you're waiting for isn't there, so the day is a bust. It almost makes you grateful for school. Is it possible that Mister Figgins is better than worrying about the mail? (The answer is no.)

I used the wait to settle a big question, at least. I definitely could be Omu the orangutan *with wings*. Why not? I used to be Dorothy from Kansas any time I wanted, and she was made up. Therefore I could make up an animal and be her and me. Actually, Dorothy is connected to Omu-with-wings. Everybody knows that *The Wizard of Oz* is the best movie ever made. It is the best movie that will *ever* be made. But the flying monkeys scare some kids. Omu isn't a monkey; she's an orange, long-haired, somewhat dopey looking – the opposite of fierce – orangutan that nobody could be scared of, even if she had wings. I wanted to make that clear.

There was no word from the newspaper yet. It was getting warmer outside, so grandpa and I began our long walks again. He liked to get outside, onto the street. It was on a walk with grandpa a long time ago, when I was a little kid, that we made the telephone poles into trees and the wires into vines. There was something comfortable about just walking around. It made it easy to talk about anything.

I hadn't talked much with grandpa about double-writing. He knew I'd entered the contest, but that was about all. He said he had something he wanted to tell me about double-writing.

"So Nora honey, you composed a piece or two for the contest. In two voices."

"Yup. Two voices like the left hand and right hand of somebody playing the piano."

"I like that. What you're doing is as much like music as like books. Instead of two notes making a musical harmony when you *hear* them at the same time, you put two words down to *read* at the same time – to make something like a harmony?"

"I don't know what to call it, grandpa. It only happens a few times. Sometimes two words at once seem to make something new. Not a third word, but something like what you said, a harmony. You stop a minute to think about it, or feel something."

"Maybe when you read only the top lines or only the bottom lines, you're getting regular sentences – prose. But maybe, now and then, when you're reading a little bit down instead of left to right, you get your moments of interesting harmony – poetry. Your pieces may be both prose and poetry."

"That would be nice, grandpa. I think what Alan wrote is like that."

"Ask him if I can read it."

"I will. I know he'll be happy for you to read it."

"Now, Nora, I want to tell you that although you invented double-writing, it was invented before. Few people know this. It's part of the history of music."

"Just like my double-writing?"

"Just like it, but sung, not read silently. Seven, eight hundred years ago, in France, a few composers wrote short pieces with two, sometimes three different texts that were sung at the same time. As interesting as the fact that they invented these pieces, is the fact that after only a few years, nobody else ever wrote them. It was as if a new and beautiful flower had bloomed, then died, and that kind of flower disappeared. You've brought that flower back. Does it make you feel bad that double-writing happened before?"

"No, no, grandpa. It's a relief, a big relief. It means I'm not nuts. Other people did it. Other other people heard it and understood it."

"I'm proud of you, honey."

"I'm proud of you, too, grandpa."

I don't know what I'd do without grandpa.

The results of the contest finally came in. I got a letter that said the newspaper was sorry but there were so many wonderful superb incredible entries, the poor newspaper couldn't give mine blah blah blah. Why do people enter contests? It's a lot like a dozen runners being in a race, but there's only one runner who really feels good at the end. The other runners feel bad because they lost the race. That adds up to one good, eleven bad. That's terrible. What kind of arrangement is that? I was mad.

I was sad too, I guess, but I tried not to be. I don't like it when strangers make you feel bad or sad. They have no right to do that. Mister Figgins had no right to make Alan feel bad *and* sad. One of my major projects is to help Alan feel *mad* instead. Anyway, mom and pop were extra nice to me. They actually expected me to feel sadder than I felt. Grandpa understood, of course. We were mad together.

Then the surprise came. A second letter. One of the people who ran the newspaper had seen my composition and liked it. It was original, he said. He said that he had a friend who was working hard for world peace and who would find my composition interesting. Would I mind if he sent it to his friend? Would I *mind?*

Alan's father had a telephone in their apartment, so I called up the newspaper and talked to the man who had written me. He was completely friendly even though I was very nervous on the telephone. That was about the third or fourth time I had used one. His friend was named Balram Desai. He was from India, but was in San Francisco at the time. Mister Stapleton – that's the newspaper person – and Balram Desai had studied politics at the University of Chicago years before. Mister Stapleton was glad that I gave him permission to send my composition to his old University friend. I think I told grandpa approximately a hundred times that a big-shot had asked my permission for something.

Mister Stapleton didn't know whether Mister Desai would have time to write to me, but he was sure that he would take what I'd written seriously. Mister Desai knew about languages that are different from English. It was possible that he was worried about language and peace the way I was. One thing was sure. My world was a much bigger place now.

Chapter Ten

Mister Desai

"What do you think, Alan? I didn't feel bad about losing the contest. Well, I did, a little, but I tried to be calm about it. Now am I supposed to be calm again, not happy because of Mister Desai and all?"

"Absolutely not calm. You can definitely be happy. Remember what we said about my nightmares?"

"That's true. 'Good dreams are good. Bad dreams are good too, even if we don't know how.'"

"Right. So you feel calm when things are bad. And when things are good, you don't have to be calm. You can be happy. What did Mister Peterson and Miss Vasquez say?"

"They said they never doubted that my composition would be recognized, whatever that means."

"It means people wouldn't think it was a baseball bat or chopped liver. They'd recognize that it was sheets of paper."

"Very funny."

"We knew most grown-ups wouldn't get it. But Mister Stapleton got it."

"Now I've got to wait again, to see if Mister Desai writes to me."

"This is a time to try to be calm, I think. Mister Stapleton said he was busy. World peace takes a lot of work."

"It's fourth marking period already and I'm not exactly the world champion fractions person. I'll kill myself over fractions; that'll distract me."

Alan's forehead got all pale.

"Don't say what you said."

"Oh rats, *rats*! What a *jerk*. I'm sorry, Alan."

"It's okay. So. How about a game of marbles?"

I didn't have to wait long at all. There went fractions. This is Mister Desai's letter.

Dear Miss Klein,

I have read your essay, "A Language of Peace," with the greatest interest. Thank you for allowing it to be sent to me.

I have often wondered why it is that we human beings are the only animals that make war. But it never occurred to me, I confess, that if we were more like animals, we might *not* make war. You propose a way to be more like animals, by writing *as* animals as well as our human selves. Added to such "doubling," as you put it, is the increase of the imagination's "heat," as you also put it. Our animal helpers and our white-hot imaginations might together hold us back from our terrible cycle of war-making. That is a remarkable idea, Miss Klein.

I should like very much to talk to you more about your ideas. I shall be leaving San Francisco for New York City in two weeks. Chicago is directly on the way. May I telephone your parents and arrange a short visit? It would be my pleasure to take your family to dinner at the Palmer House, where we can all come to know each other better.

Cordially yours,

Balram Desai

Dinner at the Palmer House!

Mister Desai must have discovered that it wasn't possible to telephone my mom and pop, because we got another note from Mister Stapleton in the mail. He would pick Mister Desai up at the airport and drive him to pop's store. This made mom nervous. "How can we entertain him in the back?" she said over and over again. It was lucky that the note arrived only two days before Mister Desai did, or mom would have got sick. I, on the other hand, was in a daze. Nora Klein the zombie.

Mom needn't have worried. Mister Desai and Mister Stapleton arrived at seven at night and seemed truly glad to see the store and meet us. Even our being crowded around our table, the six of us, worked out fine. It was like our knowing each other for a long time because our shoulders were practically touching, and the room was small, and there was a beautiful pound cake in the middle of the table big enough for twenty people, and one glass of tea followed another.

Mister Desai told pop that one of his uncles made shoes in the south of India, where he came from. "When I was a child I would trouble my uncle while he sewed, asking him questions about everything under the sun. Many people in our neighborhood came to ask him questions and for advice. He never looked up from his bench. He listened, there would be a long pause, and then he would say something in a low tone, something simple, and it always satisfied." Pop said that you didn't have to go to school to have wisdom. Honest work and caring about people gave wisdom, Mister Desai said. Grandpa said, "You bet." Mister Stapleton smiled, mom sighed, and I was Queen of the Lions, surveying her realm, majestic and full of pound cake.

Five of us would meet at the Palmer House the next night at six. Mister Stapleton would pick us up and bring us back, but he couldn't stay for dinner. He had to talk to some editor or other at six. We got dressed up, piled into Mister Stapleton's car, and met Mister Desai at the entrance of the hotel restaurant, the most beautiful room I had ever seen. It was more grand than the Palace, my absolutely favorite movie theater, the Egyptian one.

Ordering dinner was a scramble, because we had never seen that kind of menu. It was fun, though. We took chances, like explorers. I thought we were in a movie, set in Paris or Shanghai. I was a Hungarian countess who had to leave her luxurious home after a revolution. I was used to gold and diamonds, but now had to settle for regular stuff. It was fine, however, because I realized that I loved poor people. Now I was one of them, and happy for the first time. But I ordered a steak with mushrooms on top anyway, like in the old days with the dukes and duchesses.

Grandpa took a real liking to Mister Desai. He told me later that Mister Desai looked like a lively kid, a considerate young man, and a kindly old person, all at once. "He's all the people he's ever been, Nora," he said. "Many people are only the people they happen to be that day. They've lost their younger ways. Not Mister Desai. He's all there, all the time." I think I saw that, too.

All through the appetizer and the salad and the main dishes, the grown-ups told family stories. I liked hearing them. Mister Desai was one of eight children. His brothers and sisters lived in India, in Europe, and one in China. They were all interesting people, trying to make the world better. Mister Desai began as a journalist, like Mister Stapleton, then became involved in making India an independent country. His country was doing now what our own country did a long time ago, becoming independent of England. I thought that was terrific.

I even learned more about our own family. It's funny that it doesn't occur to your parents to tell you a lot about their lives, but they'll tell other people if the subject comes up. Pop said that when he was fourteen he was handed a shoemaking test. He was given a beat-up, old-fashioned boot. It was a left boot. "Make the right boot," this old shoemaker who everybody looked up to told him. "Make it so I can't tell which one you made and which one I gave you." Pop did it! Nobody could tell. I don't know why some people are called famous, but I'd call pop famous.

Pop never wanted to be anything else but a shoemaker. It's true that he was a little disappointed when he came to America; he mainly repaired shoes here instead of making them. People bought ready-made shoes in America. He didn't quite get it. "A person's left foot is different from her right foot," he always said. "It has to be made special, not on a form in a factory." But he got used to it, and mom said she didn't mind pitching in to make extra money. She wasn't with me as much as she wanted to be, but she had no doubt that grandpa did everything for me that she would do.

Grandpa didn't say much. That surprised me, because he and I talked about everything. But I suppose we didn't, not about everything. There was too much sadness in his past. The sadness didn't seem to be his personal sadness, exactly, because he's absolutely always cheerful. Mom has often told me that he was always cheerful when she was young. It was history that was sad. The time long ago when grandpa himself was young – that *time* was sad. I suppose I'll learn more about that time in school some day; then I'll ask grandpa about it. It must be that he doesn't want me to think about it now. If that's right, it's okay with me. I trust grandpa.

When we came to dessert, Mister Desai turned to me.

"You know, Miss Klein, we in India depend a good deal on our imaginations in order to make our lives more, shall I say, Indian. You possess the faith in imagination that we possess, I believe."

"People have to put themselves in other people's shoes," I said. I smiled to myself. Shoes. "If they really do that, not pretend to do that, then they wouldn't hurt other people. They would be hurting *themselves*."

Mister Desai seemed to like that. "Very logical," he said.

"Make India more Indian?" mom asked.

"Yes. You see, some of us do not think that India should become in future like other countries, Western countries. We should not build great cities like Chicago and New York. We should not depend on machines. Ancient India was a place of many villages. Grandmothers and grandfathers made the day-to-day decisions in our villages. Villagers made what they needed with their hands. We strongly believe that village-India is the true India."

"It's like you don't want to be modern," I said. I hoped that wasn't an impolite thing to say. I didn't mean it to be.

"You're precisely right, my dear. We don't believe that it is necessary to submit to every new invention that is offered us. On the contrary, in order to remain Indian, we must learn to resist much that is modern."

Pop asked how you could possibly do that.

"One of us called our method 'village-mindedness.' We put a complete picture of a traditional village firmly in our imaginations. Every decision to do something during the day is guided by that picture. A small act, then, will in its own way lead toward village India rather than away. We rely on very many acts of that kind to restore India to itself."

"In spite of the enormous cities in India as we speak?" grandpa said.

"In spite of that," Mister Desai said.

"It would be so much fun to imagine a perfect place to live," I burst out. "We could think of every way people can be happy. We could invent the best ways to do everything. We would be super-realistic, so it would all work."

"Wouldn't that be dreaming, honey?" mom said, in a nice way.

"But so many people are unhappy, mom. We *have* to dream."

"Perhaps one must be young to dream," Mister Desai said.

"Look," grandpa said, "we old guys haven't done so well. That's putting it mildly. Like Nora says, the smartest among us grown-ups haven't figured out how to end wars. Maybe we should encourage dreaming, encourage kids."

Mister Desai noticed that it had become late.

"We may be talking beyond Miss Klein's bed time, I fear, so stimulating has been our conversation. I shall call Mister Stapleton to come take you home. Unfortunately, I must be off to New York City tomorrow. I should like to propose something. We have not broached the language of peace, which is, after all, the subject of Miss Klein's splendid essay. Summer approaches. Perhaps early in July I could host your family in New York, where an unusual number of – shall I call them? – peacemakers, will be gathered. Beyond doubt the question of language and peace will be on the minds of many. Why should not Miss Klein share what she has created with them? If such a possibility interests you after you have discussed it, we can correspond about details. For the moment, I shall look for a telephone. May I say that I have enjoyed our dinner immensely."

This keeps on going, I thought: first, the school knows; then, Mister Stapleton and Mister Desai know; and now, maybe New York City and a whole bunch of Mister Desais to explain myself to. Do I like this or is it scary? Do I like this *and* is it scary? I decided it was both.

We talked it over approximately a hundred times at home. We finally decided that grandpa would go with me in July. Mom and pop didn't know New York at all, and they figured that it would be best to stay at work. Grandpa had been to New York and, as he said, had "figured it out." Alan immediately said that I'd be Captain Ridiculous if I didn't go. "Be brave, like The Human Torch," he said. (He made up Captain Ridiculous, but the Human Torch was real; there was an entire comic book about him.)

Letters went back and forth. Mister Peterson became almost as excited as I was. He and Miss Vasquez took me out for ice cream three more times before the end of school. Even George came over once at recess and told me that I was "some character." The thing was that he said it in a way that made me think he felt better that we went to the same school. I calmed myself down mainly by being Omu-with-wings pretty much every day, usually just before supper.

Swinging…swinging above everybody's heads. There's Mrs. Greenberg walking Silky on a leash. Look at Ronald and Pauly running down the sidewalk. Pauly is younger and littler than his brother but he can run just as fast. Hah, there's quite a big dog wandering around. I'll keep an eye on him. Lucky I'm strong enough to rescue him if he needs rescuing. Wait, I'm catching an updraft. I'm soaring above the buildings. Oh yes, now that I can see so much farther, there's an old man looking for his dog. Please excuse me while I reunite them.

Chapter Eleven

The Ocean

As soon as grandpa and I got off the train at Grand Central Station I asked him if we could go see the ocean. Would the ocean be like Lake Michigan? You couldn't see to the other side of the lake. The other side could be a hundred miles away or a thousand miles away for all you could tell. So how could the ocean be all that different?

For one thing, it wasn't too easy to get to the ocean in a way that would settle that question. New York City is so built up and busy and crowded and noisy that you hardly knew the Atlantic Ocean was right there. I thought the lake was more a part of Chicago than the ocean was part of New York. Grandpa and I took a taxi to our hotel, dropped off our luggage, and then rode the subway downtown to see the harbor. I think grandpa thought I was disappointed; I was, a little. What he said to make me feel better had a tremendous effect on me. "There are whales out there, Nora," he said. From that moment I absolutely loved the ocean.

It was early afternoon on the first Sunday in July. We weren't to meet Mister Desai until breakfast on Monday. Grandpa suggested that we go see the whale exhibit at the Museum of Natural History and then have supper at a cafeteria not far away from the museum. The cafeteria would remind me of the one where we had our black bread and beans, grandpa said, but this place was three times as big and served everything you could imagine. Writers and artists who didn't have much money spent a lot of their time there, talking more than eating.

What a museum! I could live there, I thought. They could put a bed someplace in a far corner, I could use the bathrooms, and there were plenty of places outside to buy rolls to eat. Perfect. I would sleep during the day while visitors were in the museum. After it closed, I would wander around becoming everything from mice to elephants. I have important things to do nowadays, so I suppose I don't really want to live there anymore, but that Sunday, life in the Museum of Natural History was the life for me.

I forgot everything at the whale exhibit. I forgot grandpa was there, that we were in New York City, what day it was – everything. I was swimming in the Atlantic Ocean.

If I ride the warm current that's rising, I can grab some air before I go down deep. There: a lung-full, and back down I go. Down... Look at that octopus. He's quite intelligent, as we know. There's not much light down here, so I can't make him out too clearly, but I can tell that he's changing colors. A fantastic thing to do, change colors. I wonder if he's thinking, and if the colors change as his thinking changes. There's the hill I particularly like. Its top is nowhere near the surface of the water, so the two-legs probably don't even know it's here. Lots of life around this hill. When there's a storm up top, all these creatures float and dart around like mad. Storms are good for the life in our ocean. Ah, time to go back up again.

"Nora? Nora, honey, are you hungry?"

"Oh, hi, grandpa. I'm starving."

"What were you thinking?"

"I was thinking I would write a letter to Alan tonight, at the hotel. One of the cards in the display cases said that whales have two places to make their sounds. Boy, grandpa, that means that *one* whale has *two* voices. Double-writing would be natural to one person with two voices if the person was a whale. Alan would be crazy about that."

"How about a celebration supper at the cafeteria, and then back to the room and a letter to Alan."

The cafeteria was steamy, just like ours in Chicago. This one was so big, and the steam was so thick, that you could barely see the walls. That was great, because you could imagine that the cafeteria went on forever. The whole world a cafeteria selling blintzes.

I had to be super-careful carrying my tray because the tables were so close together. If I dropped anything I would go up in flames for sure. We found a very good table, close to the windows. We could see a huge traffic circle and a million people hurrying around it. They may not have been going anywhere, actually. They may have just been going around and around the circle. Then my attention was grabbed by something going on a couple of tables away. I nudged grandpa to look.

There was an old man sitting there, drumming his fingers on the table. He had a plate of sour cream and a cup of coffee in front of him, but he wasn't interested in them. He was waiting for somebody. Up walks a second old man, wearing – I promise – a trenchcoat like Humphrey Bogart's, but too big. He nods. The first man nods back. Humphrey Bogart pulls out a package from his coat. The package is wrapped in brown paper, taped on every edge, and criss-crossed with rope. He looks around him in a guilty way, puts the package on the table as if what's inside it is made of glass, nods again, and walks away. An old lady comes up to the table, sits.

"He brought it?" she asks.

"He brought it," he answers.

"You haven't touched your sour cream," she says in a critical voice.

"How could I touch? This is the Busch Quartet, Rose. The Busch. The First Razoumovsky Quartet. Nobody has it. Now we have it."

"I can't wait either. Okay. Eat a little, and we'll go home to listen."

The old man eats one spoonful. Then the couple gets up, looks around, and walks out with their package.

Grandpa smiled.

"You have to love New York, Nora, even if you hate it. The Busch Quartet is the greatest string quartet in the world. The piece they named is one of Beethoven's greatest works. For the Busch to play that Beethoven is a true event. Their recording is very hard to find. Our couple seems to have found theirs in an irregular way. Not completely kosher. Somewhere else, such movements as we saw would accompany diamond smugglers. Here, a string-quartet recording. I'm telling you, you have to love New York."

What a wonderful day.

Chapter Twelve

Whale Song

We were going to be home in a week, but I knew Alan would like to get a letter. A person doesn't get that many letters.

Dear Alan,

Do you remember telling me about that canary in the apartment you delivered to last month? Samson? What a name for a bitty canary. But you said he had a Samson voice. He sang two songs at once, louder than you'd ever guess from such a little bird. Well, imagine the <u>opposite</u> of itty-bitty. <u>Whales</u> sing two songs at once!!!

There's a life, Alan. Swim all over the ocean, free up and down, back and forth, and sideways, flying but in the water instead of the air. Sing your heart out. Nobody to scare you. Shrimp for dinner.

Grandpa and I rode in the subway to see the ocean where the whales live. We didn't like the subway much. Too much noise. Grandpa says that it's not so good for a violinist, who has to protect his hearing. Then we went to a great museum where I learned a lot about whales. After supper in a wonderful place, we came back to the hotel where our luggage was. Our room is pure luxury. If you had a hotplate in it, you could live there forever. Then I wrote this for you.

We are born and live with our fellow whales.
We have songs and play and our mother sea.

We are taught about every thing around us.
We are taught that every thing has a song.

We *are* our songs.
We *are* our songs.

We become fish as children,
We swim around, playing,

Then we become huge birds.
Making believe we   fly.

We   sing their songs.
Birds *are* their songs.

We become other   whales like   us.
We sing the songs of   other   whales.

We   all   become each other.
Each of us becomes a whole clan.

When we are   very   old,
We   admire cheerful age.

We are   ready   to become the ocean
We have become larger and larger

In our imaginations.
In our imaginations.

We sing the ocean's many-voiced song.
We *are* the ocean's many creatures.

That is the   power   of our minds.
That is the meaning of our lives.

I hope you like it. Tomorrow we see Mister Desai. I'll probably be home about the same time you get this letter. Maybe I'll be home <u>before</u> you get it. Headache-ville.

Nora

Chapter Thirteen

China

Who can sleep their first night in a hotel, especially in New York City, especially if you're there to meet famous people? Grandpa and I were up and wide awake with the sun.

Being a considerate person, Mister Desai had said he'd pick us up at nine. He assumed that I like to sleep late. That's true. It just wasn't possible. So grandpa and I had a few hours to do something with. "You can only get to know a city on foot," grandpa said, so out we went for a long walk.

I had expected the streets to be a *little* crowded, but there was absolutely nobody out. The city felt eerie. No people; your only company was the silent heavy buildings. On the narrower streets, the buildings threw shadows that weighed on me. I had to get above the shadows and the buildings both. I held grandpa's hand tight and...

That's more like it. I don't see any other Canada geese up here, which makes me a bit nervous, but all in all I'm free and able to breathe. Actually, the canyons made by the taller buildings across the street from each other create fun of their own. Wind tunnels. Whoosh. I'll play in this one first. Uh oh, that cross-wind almost spun me on my axis. Wait a minute; that was fun too. I'm going back. I'm up higher than usual. The buildings here are *incredibly* tall. There's a person. The first one, and *tiny* from here. What do you know; this place is an island, and a small one. Well, they can't build any way but up, I guess. Why they want to do so much of it is beyond me. What a view of the ocean! Wow, whole flocks of pigeons. Nothing bothers them. I can go back to walking now.

"Are you okay, Nora?"

"Sure, grandpa."

"You were Beatrice? Romola?"

"Romola."

"That's good."

Grandpa knows me.

"The streets of this city either give a person energy or they suck energy right out of you," grandpa said, as more people started to appear, going to work or for breakfast. "You shouldn't live here if the streets take your energy away, because eventually you'll get sick. I couldn't live here for that reason. But I know people who *aim* for the most crowded streets. They say those places are 'electric' with energy. Not for me, they're not."

We got back to the lobby of our hotel just before nine. Mister Desai was right on time. We greeted each other like old friends.

"We'll meet Mister Chan at his hotel uptown. There's a fine restaurant there. He is eager to meet you both. Mister Chan is a scholar of the Chinese language. I took the liberty of showing him 'A Language of Peace.' He feels that you and he have much to learn from each other."

That I couldn't see. I would learn from Mister Chan, it goes without saying. But him from me? Ridiculous. But I didn't say anything. I didn't want to hurt Mister Desai's feelings.

I fell in love with Mister Chan. No kidding. He's small, maybe fifty years old, and a little chubby, and when he looks at you, you're sure that you're by far the most important person in the universe. I think grandpa fell in love with him, too. *Think* of it. Everybody he meets falls for him. He definitely goes through life differently from most of the rest of us.

Mister Desai, Mister Chan, grandpa, and I sat down at a round table set with sparkling glasses and shining plates. I ordered French toast. I will never forget that French toast, never. It was that good. While we ate, we talked about our families. Indian and Chinese people enjoy telling family stories more than anybody I ever met. When we were finished, Mister Chan asked for a paper napkin. He didn't want to write on a cloth napkin and ruin it. He drew four beautiful Chinese letters, that he called characters, in a square, and looked his fabulous look at me.

"Do you see these four ancient characters, Miss Klein? They are a poem. If one knows how to read this poem, one can read it with the greatest pleasure for an entire day, an entire year, or perhaps an entire life. It continues to produce meaning as long as you choose to gaze upon it."

I was confused. "I thought that when once you knew the meaning of a word, you went on pretty fast to the next word. Four words couldn't take all that long to read, could they? Four words in English wouldn't take very long. We're supposed to read fast."

"The meaning of each of these Chinese characters is not like a meaning that you look up in a dictionary. You are not looking for a word or two that will substitute for the word you are looking up. Instead, imagine that it is night and you are half asleep and feeling happy. You are listening to a long and wonderful story your mother is telling you. Her voice rises and falls like music. It is full of emotion. Colorful scenes of all kinds spring up in your imagination. You cannot be sure whether you are dreaming or awake. Your happiness becomes very deep. That is how it is for you when you give your attention to one of these four characters."

Everybody at the table looked as if they were in a dream themselves for a second. Grandpa broke the spell.

"That's beautiful, Mister Chan, simply beautiful."

Mister Chan went on. "Don't you, in your double-writing Miss Klein, wish meaning to expand in your reader's imagination, just as this poet wishes?"

"Oh *yes,*" I said.

"Then you, in America in 1946, and a Chinese poet living twenty-five hundred years ago, are colleagues." Mister Chan smiled like a kid.

I didn't know what a "colleague" was, and looked at grandpa.

"Like a friend and partner," grandpa whispered to me.

The question had to be asked.

"Mister Chan," I said, "did writing like this help make China a more peaceful place?"

An even wider smile. "Of course you must ask that. Yes, Miss Klein, China became peaceful in part because of such writing. You have made the connection."

We talked more about China, about how important etiquette is, about family loyalty, and about being educated so that you stay a good person. But I have to say that I don't remember much after Mister Chan said what he said – that I'd connected how you write things down to whether you live in peace. That was more than enough to think about. I couldn't fit anything more into my head.

It was a long breakfast. At eleven, Mister Chan said that it had been an honor to have had breakfast with us. He shook my hand and said that he knew I'd be back to New York. Whenever I came, I was to telephone him. In the meantime, would I send him more of my double-writing? I almost cried when he and Mister Desai left the restaurant.

Grandpa had turned down Mister Desai's offer of a ride. We weren't far from "the other museum," the Metropolitan Museum of Art. Grandpa said he had something to show me that would mean my having far-away colleagues again.

"Twenty-five hundred years ago is good," grandpa said, smiling, as we walked down Fifth Avenue. "How about five thousand years?"

Chapter Fourteen

Egypt

That is one beautiful building, the Metropolitan Museum. Inside, it was as if everything you could think of that people did to make art had a room, just like everything about nature had a room in the Natural History Museum. As far as I was concerned, you didn't have to go to school in New York City. All you had to do was go back and forth between those two museums.

The first thing we did in the museum was get lost. All the people shuffling around all the rooms made us dizzy. We saw tremendous things, but grandpa said that it was best to devote one visit to one kind of art, so he finally asked where the Egyptian collection was.

A nice guy in a uniform told us exactly what to do. We dodged bunches of kids being pulled around by teachers, bumped into a few people because we weren't always dodging fast enough, and found Egypt. It took our breath away.

There weren't many people there. You whispered, not talked. Statues looked down on us from thousands of years ago. In the shadows you imagined ghostly Egyptian people getting ready for their day or sitting at a workbench making something you've never seen before. Then I saw something even grandpa couldn't believe. On a wall – a real Egyptian wall, attached to a museum wall – a very pretty young Egyptian girl was playing two whistles at once!

"Grandpa!"

Too loud.

"Um, grandpa," I said as softly as I could without busting, "look. She has *two* whistles. Look how clever. The two mouthpieces are close together, so she can blow into them, and the other ends are farther apart, so she can get a hand on each one and put her fingers down on their holes. She can play two different songs at once! Grandpa! It's like having two throats. It's like being a whale. It's like double-writing."

I'd got loud again. How could I help it? Grandpa was as excited as I was, honestly. He said that what we'd once talked about, that many things people thought were whole things were really half-things, was true. What people called one whistle was really half a whistle. Look at clarinets and instruments like that. Were they half-instruments, and nobody knew it? Maybe one line of writing at a time really *was* half a line of writing. We were both more-or-less bouncing up and down with excitement. And there was that lovely Egyptian girl, still and silent on a wall painted longer ago than we could imagine.

"That isn't even what I wanted to show you," grandpa said. He was actually laughing with pleasure. "Well, this is reason enough for our whole trip."

"Meeting Mister Chan, too, grandpa. And the ocean full of whales."

"Of course. Those were reasons enough. This is reason enough. Some trip, and it's only Monday."

"Let's look at the girl a long time, grandpa, and then leave. So much has happened today."

"Just one more, quick thing, honey. All we have to do – after we've looked at her as long as we want – is turn around. You'll see why it's so natural to be Omu-with-wings."

Of course I had to turn around.

If what Mister Chan drew on his napkin, which, by the way, I saved and still have, was Chinese characters, then what we saw on the opposite wall was Egyptian characters. They might have been twice as old as the Chinese characters. They weren't small and delicate like Mister Chan's pen-marks on a napkin; they were thick paint on raised stone, as close to permanent as writing can get. Grandpa went close to the wall and pointed with his finger.

"See, Nora? The writer wanted to show a person who has all the characteristics of a human being *and* all the characteristics of a special kind of dog. So what did he do? He carved and painted a picture of a person with the dog's head for a head. What could be simpler than that? You want to double the meaning? *Draw* it. You want to double the meaning of Omu? Attach wings to her in your imagination. You want to double yourself? Add Omu-with-wings to yourself in your imagination. The Egyptians used their imaginations that way for more than a thousand years. That seems to me like plenty of permission for you to do the same thing, right?"

"Right, grandpa."

"I think when we're done here, we'll go back to the hotel and I'll call Mister Desai. We'll take tomorrow off. He'll understand. We have to let yesterday and today soak in. I heard on the radio while I was washing up that there's a concert tonight at a high-school auditorium downtown. A string-quartet concert – another reason to live in New York City, I confess, if you can handle the streets. We'll have a snack, take a nap, eat at the hotel, and go to the concert. Tomorrow maybe a movie, a couple of stores to find little things for your mother and father and Alan? What do you say? Back to work on Wednesday."

"You're a genius, grandpa."

I never made anybody blush in my entire life until then.

Chapter Fifteen

New York

Everything we had already done had been thrilling. The string-quartet concert was going to be a rest for us, I thought. We would unwind. Not a chance. I have to add that concert to the experiences in New York that were changing my life.

We left early so we could walk down to the school. Grandpa said that concerts at this high school were special because they were almost free, so anybody could afford to go, and because great musicians came to play for that very reason. People lined up outside the school two hours before the concert. Seats were first-come, first-served. That was fair, grandpa said. If you wanted a good seat, you should be willing to stand in line for a while. It was also very interesting to talk to the people standing near you in line.

There were already at least fifty people waiting when we arrived. We took our places, and in ten minutes there were fifty more people behind us. The first thing I noticed was that most of the people in line had gray hair. Grandpa said that the young don't always appreciate string quartets. I wondered how I would like them. I remembered the string-quartet record album in the cafeteria. Those people were old, too.

We were let into the auditorium and grandpa led me to the first row, which was filling up fast. He said that he didn't like to see the backs of people's heads at concerts. The auditorium was old and seedy, but I liked it. It smelled like wood and dusty iron. There was a growing hubbub behind us. People were finding their seats. They were whispering in an excited way. I couldn't help getting excited myself.

Grandpa took my hand, staring up at the raised stage, concentrating. Four middle-aged men walked onto the stage, two of them holding violins, one a viola, and one a cello. They sat down in a semi-circle facing us, music stands in front of them, and the lights in the auditorium dimmed. I could feel my heart thumping.

Of all the kinds of music I have ever heard, the string quartet is now my favorite kind, absolutely. Four wonderful-sounding string instruments playing incredibly great and beautiful pieces together. Four voices singing, but not quite singing. Something happens that I can't name is better than singing. I think that's it: I can't *name* what it is that's so immense about hearing a string quartet by Brahms. If I could name it, it wouldn't be as immense as it is. What happens during the music goes farther and deeper than words can go. What a mystery that is.

Never for a second did I need to add Omu, with or without wings, or Beatrice or Romola, or anyone else to myself when I listened to a string quartet. I added the *string quartet* to myself.

Grandpa kept up a continuous drone of stories about this quartet and that quartet all the way home. I was happy to listen, even if no story described what really happened. The concert had given grandpa new energy, more even than telling somebody that you play the violin either like a machine or like a human being. Myself, I couldn't think of anything more human than being inside a string quartet.

It was hard to sleep, just like it was the first night in the hotel. This time, though, I eventually dropped off and I slept late. Grandpa was already up reading the paper. We went to a coffee shop near the hotel and had pancakes. We have to be strong, fortified, grandpa said, because shopping in New York City was like football. You had to be in condition.

You sure did. We only went to two department stores and we were only looking for a few small presents, but by two in the afternoon we were exhausted. For one thing, looking at so many objects tires you out – just looking at one thing after another. Then there are the billions of people. One person bumps into you and says she's sorry. Another person bumps into you and calls you a terrible name. You catch sight of more faces than you can count, each for less than a second, but you can't help thinking *something* about every one of them. "He's so tense he's going to explode." "She's probably very nice." "She's crazy." Knick-knacks, hats, cameras, faces, *bump,* typewriters, picture frames, *bump,* faces, sweaters...

We emerged, gasping, with a flowery scarf for mom, an Enrico Caruso record for pop, a Sherlock Holmes novel for Alan, and two souvenirs for Miss Vasquez and Mister Peterson, a nice empire-state-building paperweight and a tiny very detailed Manhattan island. Grandpa said that as for ourselves, we were each other's presents.

"How about a movie?" grandpa asked. "We've got to sit down."

We saw a new movie called *It's a Wonderful Life,* with Jimmy Stewart. I hardly ever say that a movie comes close to *The Wizard of Oz,* but that one did. It was about what a bunch of people would have been like if one person, who was so sad he was thinking of ending his life, if that person had never lived at all. Those other people would have had poorer lives. When we left the theater grandpa said that the movie proved that kindness was everything. When you're kind, everyone is happier. We remembered Ronald Coleman in *Lost Horizon*. He asks this wise old man what kind of laws had made Shangri-la, which was a perfect place, so perfect. The wise old man said that it wasn't laws at all, it was kindness. Who says you can't learn big things from movies.

We took a subway downtown again. There was a restaurant grandpa remembered that served noodles in a thousand ways or more. "Noodles?" I said like a comedian, "what can you do with a noodle?" I learned that you could invent dishes the world has never seen with a noodle. After I confessed that my noodles were sensational, grandpa said that all you had to do was think like a noodle and a sensational recipe just comes to you. Very funny.

Chapter Sixteen

Africa

Mister Desai had asked us to telephone him at his office Wednesday morning when we were done with breakfast. Grandpa was still a little worried that I was being overloaded with things to think about. He kept telling me to go back to sleep, and when I finally did get up, he made a big deal about breakfast. We had to go to this famous deli downtown. We had to eat slowly. We had to take our time getting back to the hotel. It was almost noon by the time he called Mister Desai.

Grandpa explained all this to Mister Desai on the phone. The arrangement they agreed on was an afternoon meeting with the next person Mister Desai wanted me to meet, at three o'clock, in a comfortable lounge in her hotel. "No running around from one person to another," grandpa said at his end of the conversation. I guess Mister Desai had had a more exciting day in mind for me.

Well, Elizabeth Motubwa from West Africa was enough excitement for a month or a year as far as I was concerned.

Mister Desai and Mister Chan were calm people. "Serene," grandpa said. They were a pleasure to be with for a lot of reasons. Both of them smiled most of the time, in a way that made you happy to be in the same room with them. They both listened to you, hard. Most people start to listen to you, and then they begin to look bored or impatient. You know you'll have to stop talking soon or you'll lose them. That's terrible when you have more to say. Mister Desai and Mister Chan always listened to the end. Then they responded to you seriously, in detail. They remembered more of what you'd just said than you did! Most people just picked up where they left off before you spoke. There was hardly any point in your speaking at all.

Miss Motubwa wasn't what you would call merely a great listener. She *became* you. This is a huge point. I completely understand adding a real animal or plant to yourself. Beatrice, Romola, Omu, worms, lions, trees. I completely understand adding a make-believe person or make-believe animal to yourself. Alice-in-Wonderland's Alice, Oz's Dorothy, Omu-with-wings. But I must tell you, adding a real person to yourself? That's *hard*. That's what Miss Motubwa could do. That's what she did one second after I walked into the hotel lounge.

She was tall and her long dress was splashed with every bright color you could imagine. She didn't smile; she laughed. I was starting to get hungry because we'd had such a late breakfast, but I didn't show it. She immediately said that I was starting to get hungry but not showing it. Really. I stared at her. She laughed, but not at me. As far as I could tell, she laughed because she was glad to be alive. I don't know any other way to say it.

"Come, you fine young woman, your grandfather and I will take you to the hotel's best restaurant, which will cook anything you want for you. They know me."

Off we went. Miss Motubwa held one of my hands, grandpa the other. She asked me more about my composition on our way. She said that she almost caught fire when she read it. It was exactly then that I most wished Alan had been with us. He would have felt like a king. I said that I had a friend back home who did double-writing better than I did. She stopped in her tracks. "I know him!" she said in her wonderful cello voice. Grandpa and I laughed, for the same reason Miss Motubwa laughed. "I promise to send you his poems as soon as we get home," I said, sure that she already knew I would.

I actually don't remember whether I ordered food for me at the restaurant or Miss Motubwa ordered for me. By the time we sat down, we weren't separate people. The three of us ate and told jokes and laughed at the jokes and laughed for no reason. She had more stories about her relatives even than Mister Desai and Mister Chan had about theirs. The difference was that in her stories, people and animals were like me and my animals, helping each other to be happy. I felt like a fish that had been out of the water for a long time and was now back in the water. Later, grandpa said the very same thing to me about himself.

"I will be the last stranger you talk to this week, darling. Mister Desai thinks he and Mister Chan and I are quite enough for you for one visit, although he would like to see you again tomorrow. You have gone to Egypt at the Metropolitan Museum, he tells me."

When she said "Egypt," I saw the multi-colored wall with animal-headed drawings on it again. What was odd was that it wasn't just a memory, I *saw* the wall, and it was lit, as if by the sun. Miss Motubwa lit it. If there was anybody in the whole universe I knew *wasn't* a stranger, it was her.

"I speak a language, Wolof, that may be the language the ancient Egyptians spoke," Miss Motubwa said. "You have felt, I know, that your double-writing profoundly resembles Egyptian writing. You want to create additional meaning for us. Egypt wanted to create additional meaning. Listen to me. There are people from everywhere in the world in New York City now, working together to eliminate war. That is why you are here, darling. I am happy to tell you that among these people are those whose languages resemble ancient Egyptian, Wolof, and double-writing. That pleases you, doesn't it?"

"I never thought there were so many of...of..."

"'Us,' dear."

"Us, Miss Motubwa."

"Let me tell you something more of West Africa. We have a saying, 'We must feel each others' heartbeats.' This saying speaks to everything. It speaks to our inner lives, in our being each other, feeling each other's sufferings and joys, being larger than our skins. It speaks to our outer lives at the same time, to how we live with each other and help each other to live."

"It's *strong* kindness," grandpa said, "isn't it, Miss Motubwa? Stronger than what Americans or Europeans mean by kindness. It's the original kindness." Grandpa had hardly said anything the whole time the three of us were together. He was hypnotized.

Miss Motubwa got up from her chair, went next to grandpa, and stooped to kiss him on the cheek. She stroked my hair before she sat back down.

"I have a feeling about America and Europe," Miss Motubwa said. "You look to the future, think and plan for the future, every moment. Do you know that many ancient languages do not have a future tense in their languages? There is very little 'I shall, we shall, they will,' in them. A new friend of mine who lives on a Pacific Island tells me that instead of her people facing the future, they face the past. Think of it. They look before them – to the past. But not to the past that only names a year and a place and gives a little fact. They look to the imagined past of their origin, the time of their people's birth in a far distant, unique, and full time. They face a beginning, not an end, birth not death, play not work, laughter not frowns, 'I have always been alive,' not, 'I will die forever.' They are an ancient people, like my own. The modern world might wish to emulate them. Modern people would frown less, and perhaps they would find a way to peace."

The rest of the day was a blur again. I know that the three of us hugged goodbye for a long time. Grandpa and I walked to Central Park and ambled around, saying disconnected things to each other, until dark. I read once that the first human beings came from the Mountains of the Moon in Africa. I believe it.

Chapter Seventeen

Dignity

I thought I would be one of the people who grandpa said gained energy from New York's streets instead of lost energy to the streets. I was wrong. I was getting really tired by Thursday.

Mister Desai guessed that was true, especially after having talked on the phone to grandpa. We weren't due in his office until eleven. Grandpa thought having breakfast sent up to our hotel room would be like being in a movie. I knew the real reason was my energy problem.

Mister Desai greeted us enthusiastically.

"I knew that Mister Chan enjoyed our time together," he said to us, "but Miss Motubwa has simply adopted you both into her family. She dropped by after dinner and couldn't say enough about you."

Grandpa said that we felt the same about her.

"I'm going to write to her even after she goes back home to Africa," I said. "I always want to know her."

"Fortunately, Miss Motubwa will be in New York for a number of months. You have gathered that we are working to create an international organization. At the moment, under the leadership of another remarkable woman, we are putting together a document that defines the rights of all human beings. We formed a Commission on Human Rights late last year in San Francisco. The Commission is writing not far from here."

"This is wonderful," grandpa said in a low, sad voice. "After the bombings from both sides, the innocent women and children killed, the prisoners of war, the murder of Jews..." Grandpa put his head in his hands for just a second, then dropped them, put on a kindly smile, and repeated that what was happening was wonderful. I took one of his hands and didn't let go the whole time we were in the office.

"Our document will be a definition of human dignity," Mister Desai said, "whatever the person's age or sex or nationality or religion or wealth. The attack on human dignity of the last war was catastrophic. The world must define and defend what it means to be human, with all its will and resources."

"Will you protect kids especially?" I asked. "All kids are the same. They might grow up to be the different kinds of people you say, different religions and all, but when they're kids, they're the same."

Mister Desai began to say something, then stopped.

"Even though we will certainly include children in our document, perhaps we will want at a later time to produce a document about children alone. Yes. Children deserve special consideration."

Grandpa asked Mister Desai if he was satisfied with our few days in New York.

"I thought that so many remarkable people being here at the same time would make your days fruitful. As it has come about, a theme has emerged. Miss Motubwa, Mister Chan, and I have, I believe, introduced you to what I might call 'the old ways.'
They are the ways of many in the world today, and they were the ways of all the world up until the recent past. It is essential that we all understand these ways if we are to move forward to greater freedom and justice."

"They're the ways of a person's family and a person's imagination, aren't they, Mister Desai?" I said.

"Yes, Miss Klein. Your family and your imagination."

The three of us talked a while more. Mister Desai was interested in the presents we were bringing home. He and grandpa checked on the next day's hotel and train arrangements. I thanked Mister Desai over and over again. That embarrasses me a little, but I was truly grateful to him. We all shook hands and wished each other happiness.

A strange thing happened after lunch at our cafeteria. We were in midtown at a busy time of day, walking to a music store grandpa wanted to visit before we left. We were standing at an intersection waiting for the light to change. I must have been slow or not alert enough, because I was knocked onto the street, right on my stomach. I wasn't hurt at all, but what a commotion! People ran over to me, hollered for the cars to stop, helped grandpa get me up, asked what they could do, patted me on the arms. It was over in two minutes. I got a completely different impression of New Yorkers. They were fast and busy, maybe, but they were fast to be helpful too. They were dignified.

We didn't go to the music store. Grandpa thought we should bring up some good snacks to our room for later, and read. He'd had enough of the streets, he said. I had a book about dogs that I'd brought with us and hadn't looked at, and grandpa had a bunch of newspapers. We spent a quiet afternoon. Two of our favorite shows were on the radio that night. The story on one of the shows was frightening and we both shivered and loved it, and the other show had two comedians and a singer we liked. The radio made us feel at home.

We were lying in our beds, it was late, the lights were out, and we were wide awake.

"Grandpa?"

"Yes, honey?"

"You remember the Brahms quartet we heard?"

"Yes. Very well."

"You remember the part when the viola played by itself?"

"Yes."

"It sounded like mom, grandpa. It sounded like her humming me to sleep, the way she does."

"It sounded exactly like that."

"Do you think if I played the viola, you and I could play together?"

I could tell grandpa was smiling.

"We'd play like nobody's business. We couldn't be stopped."

"Could I learn to play the viola, do you think?"

"First thing we do when we get home, sweety. We'll find a viola at Stefano's. You'll have my other bow. And I'll teach you. We'll be famous."

"We'll go to Carnegie Hall."

"We'll play for Mister Truman and Mister Stalin. Your mother will wear diamonds and your father will wear a tuxedo like Fred Astaire."

"I love you, Grandpa."

"I love you, too."

Chapter Eighteen

Home

The train ride home was fun. I liked walking up and down our car. It reminded me of standing in streetcars at home, but on the train you could walk. When I walked in the opposite direction of home, I wondered whether I was going slower than the train was going. I stopped wondering after a while, though, because the problem sounded too much like something we would be asked in math class. Thought-problems give me a headache.

I first realized how much I missed mom and pop while I was on the train. In New York I hardly thought about them; I was too busy; everything was too different. It's not a good thing to be in a place where you forget people who love you. Some people probably live in New York *because* they can forget people in other places.

Grandpa and I spent all day Saturday telling mom and pop all about what we did. Pop even closed the store. He never did that. He must have missed us a lot. They asked us how Mister Chan and Miss Motubwa looked, how big the Natural History and Metropolitan Museums were, how different the ocean was from the lake, what Fifth Avenue and Central Park were like. Grandpa told them about the cafeteria and what we saw there. I went on and on about whales. The day was like living New York City all over again.

Alan had supper with us. Grandpa and I gave everybody their New York presents. We loved seeing mom and pop and Alan take off the ribbons and wrapping paper, their eyes all lit up. After supper we went to Alan's father's store, and I told him everything over again. He said that I didn't have to do that, having talked about New York all afternoon to my parents. But I wanted to. I hadn't remembered to tell about the double-whistle the Egyptian girl played, and I wanted to describe the whole plot of *It's a Wonderful Life* to him. I can take an hour-and-a-half to tell about an hour-and-a-half movie. It's a gift I have.

Alan had a surprise for me. While we were away, he read about rain forests in the branch library. He wanted to double-write about where Omu came from. What a coincidence. I was writing about the ocean at the same time Alan was writing about the rain forest. He said that he couldn't believe it when he got my poem in the mail. This is what I read in the dim light.

The morning is   quiet.
Water-drops have formed

The many-storied, wrinkled trees
Like tiny mirrors on the leaves,

Hot   at   the top,
Cool and shining.

Cool   at   the   bottom.
Form and then dissolve

 It   remains   quiet;
And then form again.

Then monkey chatter.
When the sun goes down,

Crickets and bats and cats.
All   the evening creatures

All   the evening creatures
Break into   their   songs.

Circulate   like air and   water.
They run and crawl and fly and swim,

They hardly see each other,
Their colors shades of gray.

But they know their way.

The next afternoon grandpa asked if I would like a cup of tea. He looked like he had a secret. Come to think of it, mom and pop looked that way too. They looked at me trying not to smile, then they turned away because they couldn't not smile. The four of us sat at the table, mom put cups of tea in front of us, and grandpa went into the shop to bring in what he had hidden there. Then he put a viola case on the table.

"Watch the tea," he said, and he opened the case.

First the poem, now this! I had tears in my eyes.

"We can begin tomorrow," grandpa said. "Lucky that Stefano's is open nights. We start with a few minutes a day. Holding a viola without straining a muscle is critical. It takes a long time to learn how to do that. Then scales. Nothing is better than scales. Other young musicians don't like them. Not interesting enough. Fooey. You begin a day with scales; you create the entire foundation of great music from scratch. An honor and a pleasure. You'll see. We'll be very patient, go very slowly, and still, before you know it, you and I will play the unbelievably great Duos for Violin and Viola by Mozart. You and I, Nora."

By that time I was crying pretty hard. I was laughing and crying.

Chapter Nineteen

Summer

Because I'd been in New York City, I got to know Chicago better. We have a natural-history museum, the Field Museum, and an art museum, the Art Institute, just as New York City has. The Art Institute even has lions in front of it.

Both Alan and I had a hard time getting past the main lobby of the Field Museum that summer. There are these huge stuffed elephants in the lobby. That upset Alan. He had tried to become a little more used to animals killing animals in the double-writing he'd given to me, but the sight of the elephants set him back. They had been killed, and now they were on display. The museum was full of displays like that. I decided to visit the museum by myself after July. Alan had enough to worry about without elephants.

I don't know why the elephants and the other stuffed animals didn't upset me. Their effect was different; I dreamt about them. The elephant dreams mixed up the New York and Chicago museums together. Elephants swam in the ocean like whales, their bodies under the water with their trunks above the surface, like the periscopes of submarines. Sometimes I would be perched on an elephant's back. I would shout and shout, the way Alan and I shouted at the lake in real life. I also dreamt about water buffaloes and cheetahs. I dreamt about them, but I never added them to myself while I was awake, the way I added Omu and Beatrice and the others to myself.

Alan and I passed by the Art Institute every time we walked downtown from the streetcar stop to our arcade. We'd never gone in, though. We went in three times in August, and liked it better each time. At first it was just too big, and we didn't know what we were looking at. By the third time we had a favorite place and went straight to it without getting confused by everything we saw first. The place was a room with pictures from Spain painted hundreds of years ago. I don't know why the colors and the way people were painted seemed so interesting to us. What I do know is that we could look at those paintings for a long time. We didn't feel like looking at other paintings for as long.

We made a discovery, speaking of looking at something for a long time. If you turned off the street the Art Institute was on a few blocks before you got to it, you could go to another kind of museum. I don't know what was in it, because what we couldn't take our eyes off of wasn't inside the museum. It was the front door. We stayed outside the door, looking at its small panes of glass catching the light as the sun went behind a cloud or came out from behind a cloud. The edges of the panes were cut in at an angle. Sunlight broke into rainbows behind the edges. The rainbows moved around with the changing light, criss-crossing each other. You couldn't tell where they would appear next, or how bright they would be. I wondered whether the people who built that door knew how wonderful it was. We never saw other people standing outside admiring it. They walked up to the door and opened it and went in as if there was nothing special going on.

Late summer was the best time to take the streetcar the other way, to the empty fields on the edge of the city. The dragonflies were everywhere in the air then. I hadn't gone there with Alan before. I thought he would like the yellow grass and weeds and the buzzing. He noticed that the dragonfly wings caught light the way our museum front-door glass did. The next time we went downtown to look at the rainbows, we imagined that the glass was made of dragonfly wings. That would explain the rainbows moving so much.

There were two things I needed to do every day. We fitted our trips to and away from downtown, and our movies in the neighborhood, around those two things. First, I walked Silky in the morning. That gave Mrs. Greenberg more time to get ready for the day, and I loved Silky. Alan went with us when he was up early enough. The other thing was my viola lesson.

The lesson was the last thing I did at night. Pop's machines were going until supper, and after supper I usually went over to Alan's father's shop. Grandpa liked our concentrating on music at the end of the day. You went to sleep with Bach or Brahms in your head. Grandpa always began by very slowly tuning his violin and my viola. He was absolutely right about holding the viola. It was almost impossible to do it without straining your left arm, and grandpa wouldn't let me strain anything. "You want to be able to play as long as you like when you're ninety years old? Then don't strain," he said.

All I did for the first weeks was play one note on each string. Grandpa thought that a person could do that for years instead of weeks. That's how important it was. What grandpa did to turn my long notes into real music was play the violin with me. He would create beautiful melodies over and under my one note, playing slow and fast, soft and loud. My notes were always the same, but his were always different, so the music was never the same twice. I felt like a real musician.

At the end of each lesson, grandpa took the viola and asked me to sit down and close my eyes and just listen. He would play parts of the two sonatas for viola and piano by Brahms. My favorite times became twice over my favorite times. Toward the end of August, grandpa said something I can't forget as he put the viola down.

"You know, honey, that home is you and your parents and me and the store. But home is also Brahms."

Chapter Twenty

September

There were usually two reasons to like September. Grandpa and I started going to the cafeteria again. The cafeteria was always most fun when it was colder outside. It was steamier. Second, the trees began to change color. That was usually about it for September. Everything else was connected with school.

This September, though, followed the summer of double-writing and New York City. Even before school started, grandpa got a letter from Mister Stapleton about New York City. He didn't think it was exactly fair to have a story in his newspaper about somebody who lost the newspaper contest but then went on to have such an unusual experience because of the contest. The winner of the contest might feel bad. I completely agreed with that. But he did think more people would like to know about my conversations with Miss Motubwa, Mister Desai, and Mister Chan. His idea was to ask a friend of his who was a professional writer but didn't work for the newspaper to talk to me. His friend would write something about my double-writing and grandpa's and my visit to New York. Mister Stapleton was sure that a particular magazine he had always liked would publish what his friend wrote.

Grandpa asked me if I would like to talk to Mister Stapleton's friend. I said I would if he would. We thought, like Mister Stapleton, that other people would be interested in the conversations since they were about making a world that was at peace. There were already stories in newspapers and magazines about a world-wide organization in New York that would be devoted to a peaceful world. A story about a sixth-grader in Chicago who cared as much about peace as grown-ups did might be interesting for grown-ups to read.

A very nice middle-aged lady named Agnes Kelly, Mister Stapleton's writer friend, came to our store a few days after grandpa telephoned Mister Stapleton at the newspaper. Mom baked a loaf of her famous rye bread for bread and butter and tea. We all sat around the table, and for the fourth or fifth or millionth time, grandpa and I told about our week in the City. Miss Kelly took pages and pages of notes. She didn't have to ask many questions because grandpa and I had become pretty good at describing our conversations. When we were done, she asked a couple of questions that stumped me. I asked her if I could write my answers to her after I had talked more with my family and teachers and Alan. They were questions I hadn't thought about.

Miss Kelly asked me what the "meaning of the week" was for me. What would I do now that was different? Had I been so changed by the week that I now had "new purposes?" I thought, Do kids have purposes? Miss Kelly was happy to give me a week or two, since she would be putting the story together during that time. She'd even come back to the store to talk, so I wouldn't have to spend a lot of time writing when there was schoolwork to do. She said that I "needed some distance" on New York. I had my own definition of distance. I've caught updrafts between tall buildings, but I've never flown as high as this. It's a little harder up here. The air feels thinner, so my wings are moving more of it, and there are some surprisingly strong gusts. I'll bank toward that steady wind so that I can continue flying out over the lake. There. Up, up... I need to get as high up as I can, so that I can see the farthest. The higher, the farther. Look at that, the backs of lower-flying geese. I can think up here.

"I do feel different because of that week," I said to Alan, "so I *should* do different things. But what?"

Alan said that he had been thinking about that himself.

"Some of what you should do is the same as what you *have* been doing, Nora. You should keep on adding animals and stuff to yourself. You should keep on double-writing. My guess is that what you should do that's new is tell people about it all."

"Why should they care?"

"Because of what you say, because they want a peaceful world."

"But I can't tell grown-ups what to do. I can't tell kids what to do."

"That's true. You have to talk to people, but not tell them what to do."

"How do I do that?"

"I'll think more about it. Ask your grandpa and your mom and pop. School starts Tuesday; ask Mister Peterson."

I did ask grandpa and mom and pop. I have to say that they were a little stumped, too. They were very interested, though. Pop said that politicians are always telling people what to be or what to do, and that's no good, even if we *do* elect them. He said that parents do that to their children, but parents love their children, and children need to be protected. Mom agreed. She thought that one of the hardest things a parent has to do is know when to *stop* telling their children who they were. Grandpa had a good idea. He thought you could teach people how to ask *themselves* what to do. There were ways to do that, he said. I couldn't think of any.

I was glad to see Mister Peterson again. It was nosy of me, but I asked him how Miss Vasquez was. He blushed. That was the second time I made an adult blush. He said she was fine, and she was looking forward to the three of us going to Anton's now that school had begun. I said that maybe we could go soon, because I had an important question for them. Mister Peterson was eager for that. He wanted to hear about the New York City week. And I still had their presents.

Chapter Twenty-One

Anton's

Two people can agree about a big thing, but disagree about a little thing that's inside the big thing. What I mean is, Alan and I agree that the world's most perfect food is a chocolate sundae. How could a person not know that? But Alan says that "a chocolate sundae" means whipped cream on top of the chocolate. I say that vanilla ice cream and chocolate syrup are a chocolate sundae, period. Whipped cream is extra. I don't like whipped cream. So Alan and I disagree about that. We had a good plan for the times only the two of us went to Anton's. We both asked for whipped cream, and I gave Alan mine. I'd be happy, and Alan would be extra-happy.

When Miss Vasquez, Mister Peterson, and I went to Anton's, I asked if they would like extra whipped cream. Miss Vasquez said she loved whipped cream, so I ordered my sundae with whipped cream and gave it to her. It's kind of a good system, I think. When the sundaes came, I also gave Miss Vasquez her empire state building paperweight and Mister Peterson his model Manhattan island. They said that they liked their gifts very much.

I began to tell about New York City. When I talked to Miss Kelly, I mainly described my conversations with Miss Motubwa, Mister Desai, and Mister Chan. I left out some of the other things grandpa and I did because I didn't think Miss Kelly would be interested in them. But at Anton's I mostly talked about those other things. I was pretty sure that Miss Vasquez and Mister Peterson would think that Egypt was as important to the meaning of my week in New York as the conversations were.

"The Egyptian girl, Nora," Miss Vasquez said, looking extremely serious, "she played two long whistles at once? We take for granted that we speak one word at a time, I suppose because we only have one throat, as you say. The double-whistle *divides* one throat into two, and two different *notes* can be played at the same time. I'm saying this so I can see it. Your double-writing gives a reader two different *words* at the same time. The Egyptian double-whistle serves our ears; your double-writing serves our eyes. My goodness, Nora. It seems that we humans can absorb more with our ears and eyes than we thought we could."

I said that whales could do what the Egyptian girl did, without anything extra to help them. They sang two melodies at once and heard two melodies at once. Why couldn't we be more like whales?

"I suspect that whales are fairly peaceful too," Mister Peterson said. "Some of them have sharp teeth and all of them are large and powerful, but they don't rampage through the oceans killing each other."

"Maybe they get everything out," I said. "Maybe they sing out everything that's inside them, but *we* don't know how to talk out everything that's inside *us*."

"And double-writing can help us do that," Miss Vasquez said, still thinking hard.

I told them about the string-quartet concert grandpa and I went to.

"When you can see the four people playing different notes on their instruments, you can hear the notes better," I said. "I think that helps you let more of the music inside yourself. Like you said, Miss Vasquez, people can hear more than they think they can hear. Hearing more makes you happy."

"Here's a question," Mister Peterson said," are happier people more peaceful people? If whales get more of what's in their minds out for other whales to hear, and those other whales can actually hear it, and if all that makes whales happier, is that why they're peaceful, or one of the main reasons they're peaceful?"

Miss Vasquez didn't see why people couldn't be more like whales. She said that we're both, whales and us, big smart mammals. They're the ones in the water; we're the ones on land. So we on-land mammals had to learn how to get what's inside our heads out into the air, and how to hear it all so we can be more happy. Maybe that would go a long way toward being peaceful. Peace in the water, peace on land.

"You said that the meaning of the week in New York had to give you something new to do back in Chicago," Mister Peterson said to me. "Then you can tell Miss Kelly what that meaning is, and you can start doing the new thing. Well, first, how about your telling Miss Kelly what you learned in New York, that people can say more and hear more, and that's a very good thing. And second, you can start thinking about how you can teach people *how* to say and hear more."

"A teacher of happiness," Miss Vasquez said. "I'll bet that your learning to play the viola is also learning how to get more of your feelings out for other people to hear."

"And for yourself to hear, too," Mister Peterson added. "Sometimes we don't *know* that we feel something until we hear ourselves *express* that feeling. It's a circle. I feel something and then express it; I express something and then I realize that I feel it."

We talked like that for an hour. I thanked them for my sundae and all the help they gave me. They really were helpful, but there was a problem. I didn't want to teach anybody anything. I couldn't say that to two teachers! There was a solution to the problem, though. Maybe I could help some people help each other to say more and hear more. No teacher, no students. Just people figuring out how to help each other do those two things.

That's what I told Miss Kelly. She seemed pleased, and said that she would finish writing the story in a few days.

I was truly excited to go to school the next day. I had my new thing to do.

Chapter Twenty-Two

The Peace Club

Room 12B at school has a beat-up round table in it. The seven of us can sit around it without anybody being "at the head of the table." Ten minutes before we were to meet for the first time, I put a sheet of paper in front of every chair. This is what was on the paper.

The Peace Club

We are all equal. There is no leader and there are no followers.

1. **Listen** very hard to the person who is talking. Wait until the person is finished. What you say next should be about what you just heard.

2. **Help** the person who is talking to say everything the person wants to say. It is hard to say everything you mean.

3. **Talk** should always be thoughtful – "thoughtful" meaning "full of thoughts" and "thoughtful" meaning "considerate."

4. **Why** we are here is to help the world be <u>less mean and more kind.</u>

The Peace Club was Alan and me, George and his sister Patty, Jerome, Louise, and Marilyn. I hoped George didn't sign up to make fun of us.

We were all sitting at the table looking at the rules by ten after three. Everybody looked at me to say something, but I didn't speak. I smiled at everybody, but didn't say anything. Nobody else did either. Twenty after three.

George   What's going on?

Alan   Nobody knows what to say, George.

Louise   Okay. I'll say something. Make the world less mean? Less mean to who?

Patty   I can tell you that. Less mean to kids. Everybody's mean to kids.

Marilyn   And less mean to people who look different.

George   What do you mean?

Marilyn   I look different to white people because my skin is brown. I can tell when they look at me, a lot of them. They don't like me. That's mean. They don't know me.

Me   Kids and people who look different.

Jerome   Are you making a list?

Me   Yup. Is that okay everybody?

	Why not?
	Okay.
Everybody	Sure
	Yah.
	Make a list.
	Go ahead.

Alan   More people who people are mean to?

Jerome   People who talk different?

Me   Absolutely, Jerome. Snobby people look at you as if you should vanish from the earth if you say the wrong thing or say something in an accent or something.

Louise   You said, "say the wrong thing." How about people who are mean to people who *think* different?

Marilyn   Like how?

Louise   Well...like a different religion from yours.

Marilyn   *You're* not kidding.

Alan   Boy, kids and looking different and talking different and thinking different? Don't people like *different?*

Patty   Can I ask about the other thing? "More kind?" Less mean and more kind?

Jerome   Kind is being nice.

Louise   But how do you know *how* to be nice, and if you're nice *enough?*

Me   I think you have to imagine you're in the other person's shoes.

George   Yah, that's what I thought you'd say.

Patty   See, George? you just put yourself in Nora's shoes!

It took us a little while to get started, and then we had a really hard time stopping. That's what convinced us that we had a true club. We would meet every week and pick up where we left off the time before. At the end of this first meeting, we thought different ones of us could pick one meanness from our list; we had more than seven kinds of meanness in only a half hour. Then we would have an expert, sort of, on each kind. Maybe we'd have a separate meeting for each kind of meanness. We would end each meeting by trying to figure out how being mean in that way could be stopped

I asked George if he was going to stay in the club. He said he would give us a chance. That was his way of saying yes.

Chapter Twenty-Three

In Which It's Not Just One Club

I was Beatrice flying medium high over the neighborhood.

Look, there's a mom walking with her kid. He's about three years old. Oh, see that? The kid found a stone on the sidewalk. It has two or three different colors. He's sitting down to look at it. The mom is pulling his arm. "Get up." She's in a hurry. But it's more important that he looks at his stone. He's crying. His mom is telling him to stop. You can't just stop, like that, click, I stopped. He has a reason to cry.

I'm turning left at the light. Two eight- or nine-year-olds are bouncing a tennis ball back and forth. What are they doing exactly? They're stooped facing each other, two sidewalk-squares apart. The ball has to be hit into the other person's square, as if the line separating the squares was a net. They're hitting the ball softly. Oh, I understand. They're not trying to *win,* by hitting the tennis ball hard so the other kid can't return it. They're trying to *keep the game going,* by hitting the ball so that the other kid *can* return it. They like to play, not win. Smart kids.

Oh no! I think that man is going to hit his little girl! I'd stop him if I could. I'd stop his arm and sit him down and talk to him for a week or a month or a year. *You can't hit!* I'm going up, up over the buildings and over the clouds. I have to think. I have to figure out how to stop people from hitting.

The day after the first Peace Club meeting I telephoned Miss Kelly to tell her about it. She said that she would like to describe the meeting in her story for the magazine. Would I mind if she added that I would like hearing from people? I said that I would like a lot to hear from people. They might think of things the Club hasn't thought of.

The story about New York and the Peace Club came out in the November issue of *America.* It was called, "Nora Klein and World Peace." I liked the story, but was embarrassed by the title. At least there wasn't a picture.

The first letter I got about the story was from Miss Motubwa. She'd written me when school started to say how much she liked our time together and to wish me a good beginning to seventh grade. Her second letter was about my project.

Dear Nora,

     I knew that you would continue to do wonders. The more I think about your double-writing, the more I see it as a return to the power of hieroglyphics, a return to Egypt and to Africa, a return to feeling the other's heartbeats. So of course you would create a way for your entire society, in which it becomes more difficult daily to feel each other's heartbeats, to return too.

     Peace Clubs will blossom like spring flowers, bringing hope to those whose lives have been too long in winter. Let me suggest one small thing, Nora dear, for you to think about. Perhaps now and then, a Peace Club can invite grandparents too? The quite young and quite old belong together, don't they? After all, it has been those in the middle who have made much of the world's trouble.

     I send you crushing hugs and juicy kisses.

Your lifelong friend,

Elizabeth

People I didn't know began to write to me.

Dear Miss Klein,

     I am writing to thank you for your Peace Club idea. I thought that you would be interested in how a group of seven adults is working out its own Club. We divided the terrible world of violence into seven regions: violence toward children, women, the poor, people who are not white-skinned, and nature, and violence among nations and among religions. Each of us will write a short essay in two parts. The first part will describe the history of the particular violence; the second part will suggest remedies for the particular violence. We will discuss one essay each month. After seven months, we will decide what we might do next. As you can see, we were inspired by your Club at school.

The seven of us are very enthusiastic about our Peace Club. We feel that we can make a genuine contribution to reducing violence in the world. You have done us a very great service in starting us out.

Sincerely,

Gerald Wilson, M.D.

Grandpa was especially pleased by that letter.
This came from a kid in Burlington, Vermont.

Dear Nora Klein,

Hello. My name is Norman Gray. I am in 7th grade. I have read the story about your Peace Club in the American magazine. I think Peace Clubs are a very good plan.

You think that one line of writing should be two lines. How about this idea. One person in a Peace Club should be two persons.

Every time Joe says something at a meeting, Fred continues on with Joe's thought out loud. He asks Joe if the whole thought is now out in the open. Every time Fred says something, Joe does the same thing for Fred. Nobody else can say anything until each person's helper is finished helping. So a Peace Club with eight people in it actually has four Peace-Club-people in it. Everything you want to say will come out because you have a helper, and every time you help your helper, you practice what the story says, adding somebody else to yourself.

Thank you for reading this.

Sincerely,

Norman Gray

I wrote back right away.

Dear Norman,

What a great idea! Our Peace Club will meet as separate people a few more times, then we'll meet as two double-people and one triple (there are seven of us). At the end of the year we're going to invite some grandparents to join the Peace Club. Then we'll get to an even number of people, so we'll have pairs of helpers with nobody left over.

I'll write to you again.

Sincerely,

Nora

More kids wrote to me, from Vermont and Rhode Island and New York, about starting Peace Clubs in their schools. I had no idea whether Peace Clubs would spread very far, but I hoped they would. The more of us the better.

Chapter Twenty-Four

Grandpa

"Grandpa?"

"Yes, honey?"

"Are you going to die?"

"Someday, yes."

"I don't want you to die."

"I know. But I'll tell you something. You're teaching me how to do it right when the time comes."

"Me? Teaching you?"

"Absolutely. See, Nora, an old guy like me worries that somebody he loves will feel too sad for too long after he dies. He doesn't want somebody he *loves* to be that hurt. He would die *really* sad if he thought he was leaving such sadness behind. So. You know how to add a bird or a tree to yourself, right?"

"Yes."

"You're working on adding a person, which, we're surprised to learn, is hard to do."

"Yes."

"Before I die, you'll add me to yourself."

"I will, grandpa, I *will*."

"I'll be happy then, because after a little while you won't be less than you were before, you'll be more; you'll be you-plus-me. It will be a while, because when you're sad you're sad, but that will pass, or an important part of it will pass, and you'll have a hundred years of being both of us."

"You'll be happy when you die?"

"Yes, honey."

"Can we face the special past Miss Motubwa told us about whenever we can, instead of the future, where death is?"

"Your viola can take you there, Nora. The viola isn't only the voice of your mother. It's the voice of mother earth herself. The craftsmen who invented the viola long ago did it so they could hear the voice of mother earth. Mother earth is who Miss Motubwa was talking about. When you play your viola, you face the special past."

Grandpa gave me an extra-long viola lesson. I was now putting my first finger down on the strings. He wrote easy, wonderful melodies for me to play as he played his great swoops and runs on his violin. After the lesson he played the opening of Beethoven's twelfth string quartet – one violin sounding like two violins, viola, and cello. I couldn't believe it.

It was late. Mom and pop were long asleep. (They said that my lessons were like lullabies for them.) Grandpa said he'd make tea.

"We talked about the special past, Nora. That past is about life and mother earth. The regular past, that you read about in history books, has often not been about life. You remember what Alan's father told you about his wife, Alan's mother. Years before their tragedy, to the east of their village in Europe, my own Ruth, your mother's mother, was...was..."

"It's okay, grandpa. Don't go on. Don't cry." I was crying too.

Grandpa recovered himself.

"I wandered a long time with your mother, the two of us, when she was a baby. We walked east, across Siberia. We met with kindness, and also with hatred. Hatred of a baby, Nora. We finally found ourselves in a place called Kamchatka, where we found a boat that was to cross the Pacific Ocean to California. I was able to teach in California, philosophy and history in a college for a while. I gave up teaching. History and philosophy had become painful to me. We continued our wandering east, across America. Your wonderful father, a great man, Nora, settled us here in Chicago. Now, you are my teacher. What you have done has made me more happy than I thought I could ever be again after my Ruth's death."

I couldn't say anything. We finished our tea and went to our beds, to look up at the ceiling in the dark, images and images passing above us.

Chapter Twenty-Five

True Love, Continued

I went out a lot that first winter of our Peace Club. Grandpa and I decided to go to our cafeteria every Friday to celebrate the end of the school week. It's a great meal, beans and bread and coffee. They go together in a mysterious way. I convinced grandpa that I could handle a little less milk and sugar in my coffee in view of my racing toward becoming a teen-aged person. He asked me if that meant he had to call me Miss Klein. I said that Her Highness Miss Klein would be more suitable.

Alan and I also went downtown more often, because of our museums as well as our arcade and our hollering into the lake. That was sometimes hard on us, because the wind on Michigan Avenue, which always practically knocked us over, also practically froze us to death that January and February. On the other hand, the worse the weather, the greater the triumph. Our raw courage was legendary on Michigan Avenue – to us, anyway. We had our donuts and black coffee on the coldest days. They were our rewards for unbelievable bravery.

Treats with Mister Peterson and Miss Vasquez became a regular thing. Alan now came with us every time. Mister Peterson and Miss Vasquez said that now that neither of them was a teacher of ours, the four of us should consider ourselves more as friends than as teachers and students. They insisted that I had more to tell them than they had to tell me. I kept them up to date on the letters I wrote to Miss Motubwa, Mister Desai, and Mister Chan. The news from New York was about the document that was being written about human rights, whoever and wherever human beings were. The document was coming right along. The news *to* New York was about our Peace Club and about the Peace Clubs popping up in other places, and I sent on Alan's and my double-writings. Alan and I also reported on our Peace Club to Mister Peterson and Miss Vasquez. They said that they would form one themselves in the spring. They already knew several teachers who wanted to have a Club of their own.

There were other plans for the spring.

How could Mister Peterson and Miss Vasquez *not* fall in love? Mister Peterson was already goofy about Miss Vasquez last year. The main thing, though, was how kind they were to each other, all the time. It was fun to watch. Each would ask the other one what would be good to do, and they would go back and forth for a thousand years to make sure that the other one *really* wanted to do whatever it was. Alan and I were talking about it once and we had a flash at the same time: the back-and-forth part was more important than the decision to do the thing. Alan had said that what they did wasn't efficient, and then we both laughed and blurted out that love is the *opposite* of efficient.

They decided to get married in the spring. Naturally, Alan and I thought starting up a Peace Club in the spring was *much* more serious than getting married, but there's no accounting for how grown-ups think.

I was pretty close to being too busy in late winter. School wasn't all that easy, and now there were letters to read and to write on the weekends. I didn't count viola lessons as part of being busy, because they were like eating and sleeping. What with school and keeping Alan's father company and going downtown and going out with Mister Peterson and Miss Vasquez and Fridays at the cafeteria, what suffered was movies. Alan and I solemnly swore that when we were old we would go to the movies twice a day.

The wedding would be during spring vacation. Mom, pop, grandpa, and Alan's father were invited as well as Alan and me. That was a considerate thing to do. There were lots of preparations. Poor Alan had to have all new clothes because of a growth-spurt. He was very annoyed. I already had good stuff. Mom had hardly worn the scarf grandpa and I gave her. The flowers on it were light blue and dark blue, so she found a shimmering dress downtown in those colors to wear with the scarf. Pop was like me; he didn't have to buy anything. Grandpa said that he personally looked like Gary Cooper in anything he put on, so there was no need for him to be concerned about clothes.

What a happy wedding it was. The bride and groom's families came to Chicago from all over. Teachers were there with their husbands and wives and kids. I remember someone saying that some weddings don't like to have children at them. At this wedding there were as many children as adults. So you heard laughing and crying and hollering and music, but mainly the laughing, of happiness. Alan and I had a small surprise ready.

We knew that the best man would make a toast to the bride and groom. The second it was over, I stood up at our table, shaking. "Alan and I would like to propose a toast too," I said. I'd rehearsed that at home quite a few times. Alan stood up. We read this aloud together, Alan taking the top line, me the bottom line – the first time any of our double-writing became double-speaking.

"This is what we wish for you.
"This is what we wish for you.

That for all   of your *life*
You   will feel growing *love*

You will both feel and *think*
And for that, each will *thank*

Together. *Hooray!"*
The other. *Hooray!"*

What Ought To Be Done

One

Childrearing

I.1 The British psychiatrist Ian Suttie said that the setting we create for our children is either one of power or of tenderness. Suttie called the leading feature of modern times the "tenderness taboo." The tenderness taboo must be lifted, or we will continue actively to build a failing society.

At this writing the Equal Rights Amendment lacks only three states before becoming the twenty-eighth Amendment to the Constitution. The twenty-ninth Amendment should stand to children as the ERA stands to women. An Equal Protection Amendment must guarantee that the protections of adult assault law will be extended to all children from birth.

I.1.1 Following the EPA being moved in the House or Senate, the Surgeon General's Office would launch a nationwide educational program demonstrating the necessity of stopping the corporal punishment of children. Research from several directions – neuroscientific, developmental, and sociological among them – has established the necessity unequivocally. First, the research would be summarized and widely disseminated. Second, non-violent methods of childrearing would be described fully and clearly, giving particular attention to stressful situations in and away from home. The orientation of the educational program would be one of care and helpfulness toward parents as well as tenderness toward children.

I.1.2 Following the passage of the EPA, traditional and non-traditional social services must be expanded. A considerable expansion of the training of psychiatric social workers will be necessary, for example, in order responsibly to intervene in homes where children are being struck.

A word about taxation is appropriate in connection with such matters as the expansion of social services. Realistically to save American society means that we must save capitalism and democracy, both institutions having revealed serious flaws. Financing expanded services – and indeed saving capitalism – requires a genuinely graduated income tax, immune to the manipulations of the powerful. Thus a "social capitalism." The rescue of democracy, the subject of **IV** below, is a more complicated problem.

I.2 We must continue to work toward universal single-payer healthcare, financed entirely by a corrected graduated income tax, in this first instance so that all children receive the preventive and corrective attention they deserve.

I.3 Parental leave must be removed from the whim of employers and states and made available to all parents. Leave should be of two-years duration, at full pay, return employment guaranteed. We now know from neuroscience that the right-brain to right-brain, tactile, pre-verbal, and verbal communication between mother and child is essential to the child's lifetime possession of the empathy that makes a humane society possible. This is a consideration that cannot be compromised.

I.3.1 Recourse to daycare facilities must be discouraged, by the argument of **I.3** above. Regarding the fewer such facilities permitted licenses, all remaining daycare employees must have the same credentials as the new body of social workers mentioned in **I.1.2**.

I.3.2 In order to encourage extended-family settings – as distinguished from nuclear-family settings – for childrearing, tax incentives should reward the convergence of distantly housed family members. Where possible, the purchase of a larger home or the renting of nearby apartments in which relocated family members can live should be encouraged. Being raised by grandparents, uncles, aunts, and cousins helping the mother and father is the oldest and longest-lived of humane settings for the beginning of life.

I.4 E.B. White said before World War Two that television would be the test of the twentieth century. We have failed that test.

A thought-experiment. Imagine that a twenty-first-century American family feeds its children chocolate cake and orange soda exclusively. The children want the cake and soda; they sincerely do. The parents say that they, the hard-pressed parents, have no choice: "The kids say they want it, so we give it to them." The children become sick. Let us say that the GDP grows because of the success of the chocolate-cake and orange-soda businesses. A think-tank publishes a study arguing that not only does the economy benefit from the growth of these enterprises – perhaps the economy *depends* on their success – but the hard-won American tradition of freedom itself calls for the defense of the parents' right to choose their children's diets. Would we do something?

Of course we would do something. We would intervene. We need only use our common sense. Children need real food.

Legislative intervention must limit what appears on television. Television is universal cake and soda rationalized in bad faith, and our children are sick.

What of First Amendment protection? Here we have a consequential instance of the difference between the eighteenth-century setting in which the Constitution was conceived and the present day. A popular culture that enriches itself on the packaging of hysteria and celebrations of violence and stupidity – contents by no means new to American popular culture – has only recently been made available in high-decibel saturated color to every single child and adult in America, continuously. That is new. In the 1960's the dangers that television posed to children were demonstrated in university-sponsored research. In 1970 a distinguished and disinterested panel brought together by Senator John Pastore of Rhode Island concluded that television programming was harming our children. Senator Paul Simon of Illinois collected hundreds of studies confirming the Pastore report through the 1980's. There were no disconfirming studies. In the 1990's and in the new century the American pediatric institution has warned against putting babies and toddlers in front of screens. For all this, programming has steadily become more tawdry, and both the national IQ and the national empathy quotient have declined. This is not so much a First Amendment question as one of criminal child-abuse and the decline of American society. Congress and the Supreme Court must rise to the occasion.

Two

Education

II The American public-education system is a failure. Our economic and political systems are damaged but reparable; our educational system must be entirely re-thought. What follows is designed to preserve – in the case of unloving households, to create – childhood pluri-potentiality and happiness, to appreciably increase competence and creativity, and to build national and world community.

Nine strands run through Kindergarten through 12th grade.

II.1 Music. Children are encouraged to sing from the age of five. Present-day schools silence children. Soon they are taught how to sing together; each class becomes a chorus. At seven or eight, they take up the Flutophone, a brilliantly thought-out instrument that is far easier to learn to play than the recorder. Soon each class becomes a Flutophone orchestra. At ten, the children are encouraged to choose the violin, viola, cello, or piano. At seventeen, many children are playing Mozart piano quartets among other masterworks of Western music.

II.2 Dance. Children begin by hopping and skipping to drum rhythms. Present-day schools tie children down. Soon they are taught dances from around the world – their introduction to other cultures. At seventeen, most children are expert tangeras, tangeros, and waltz partners

II.3 Making things: art and use. Children begin by finger-painting and playing with clay. At seventeen, they are working in oils, stone, wood, and paper, making both art and objects of use. It is made clear that at the very least we all possess a strong intelligence of the hands as well as an intelligence of the head.

II.4 Stories: talking, reading, and writing. At first, children are told stories from all the parts of the world that are providing them dances. Soon they are telling stories to each other. Present-day schools, having silenced children, leave them to learn how to talk to each other elsewhere – a splendid opportunity lost. Soon children ask to learn how to read so that more and longer stories can become available to them. Then, just as they first are told and then tell stories, they begin to write stories once having read them. Soon they add writing arguments – see **II.5** upcoming – to writing stories. At seventeen, the children are likely to love literature.

II.5 Logic and mathematics. The most important pedagogical breakthrough in modern curricular history was made by the School Mathematics Study Group in the 1950's. By the mid-1960's at least one K-12 sequence based on the SMSG was commercially available. For unfortunate reasons the work of the SMSG was dropped, and school mathematics returned to its dreary past practices. When we return to the SMSG materials, we will find that creativity in finite mathematics and the mathematical sciences will explode. Having begun at five by drawing small circles inside then outside bigger circles, at seventeen surprisingly many children will be adept at differential equations.

II.6 American Sign Language. It is imperative that children internalize the two senses of "symbol." The first sense belongs to **II.5** above and represents a spectacular achievement of modernity. If this first sense implies precision, then the second sense implies plenitude. In order to absorb the second sense, which is a spectacular achievement not of modernity alone but of all human history, all children should learn a second kind of language – not a "second language" but a second *kind* of language. ASL is such a language. Not surprisingly, children love learning it. At seventeen, they will be adepts.

II.7 Nature. Children will begin not as scientists but as naturalists, out of doors, and they will stay naturalists. Later they encounter the natural sciences, and regard them as subsets, based on observation and analysis, of their original and larger love of nature, based on observation and admiration.

II.8 Cooking. Absolutely. All children should learn to make tasty, healthy, ingenious meals. They soon make their own lunches at school. At seventeen they are rivaling Escoffier.

II.9 The capstone. All children take care of living beings. They learn how to keep plants and animals alive and well, and they do this throughout their school lives. The chances become good that they will continue to take care of plants and animals, each other, and the earth throughout their lives.

Three

Economics

III The creation of a free public educational system in Great Britain in the nineteenth century was a response to the expansion of the franchise. Back then there was little need to misrepresent the reason for public education: it was to guarantee a compliant electorate. Democracy was not to be permitted to hamper the rule of the few. The situation was somewhat different in the United States early in the twentieth century. Thinkers like John Dewey wanted the full development of American children to be our reason for a public system. Some of that stuck, but over time, the nineteenth-century rationale prevailed. Of course the rhetoric of full development was retained. If, in the twenty-first century, we pick up where Dewey left off, we will save our society.

III.1 In the degree that a public-educational system resembling the one described in **II** is installed, the world of work will change. The siphoning away of the imagination and the laying down of resignation as the mechanism for coping with adulthood, both products of the present system, having ended, young adults will move into the economy with expectations of fulfilling work, and they will possess the internal means for finding or making fulfilling work. It is a pitiable thing to look at a society in which the best energies of too many of its inhabitants are given to life-long mind-numbing or otherwise death-dealing work. The provisions of **I** and **II** above are designed to change that state of affairs. Our economy will be subsumed to our fulfillment as human beings.

III.2 We know that societies in which the gap between the rich and poor closes are exactly those in which economy is subsumed to fulfillment. The United States is far down on the list of fulfillment societies. The gap between our rich and poor is too great. The graduated income tax that we have already seen protecting our children is the appropriate mechanism for reducing that gap.

Four

Politics

IV In modern times, rule by the few has too often depended on persuading the many that the many rule. Whole rhetorical institutions – advertising agencies and media empires beholden to a small number of corporations with little interest in the public good – are created to effect such persuasion, and they tend to succeed. One of the baleful results of this political fact is that far too many ambitious and insubstantial aspirants to political power obtain it. Essential to the rise of such people to power is the commandeering of money. So the first remedy that comes to mind is a simple one: stop the flow of money into politics. There is a far more complex problem, one for which no solution, simple or not, has surfaced. How, in our representative democracy, do we the people obtain the best representatives?

Ultimately we must rely, first, on compassionate childrearing as assisted by **I.1.1,** and second, on a free universal education that cultivates all human capacities rather than a small selection of them, on a model resembling **II.1-9,** so that an electorate fully capable of self-rule comes into being. But the question of keeping the wrong people out of power and finding the right people to exercise power should be joined right away. This is an appropriate task for our universities. Broadly constituted panels should examine a far wider array of political solutions than is now available for serious consideration. Should a democracy create an examination system, for example, aimed at identifying the gifts a representative of the people should possess? What are those gifts? A high-spirited national conversation is overdue.

Five

Social Relations

V Let us say that our childrearing and our public-educational systems have become more humane, that the gap between our rich and poor has significantly closed because of the perfecting of our graduated income tax, that work has become more personally satisfying and socially responsible, and that the right people are ensconced in local and national government. These would be causes for an over-all feeling that our society is a fit one in which to live. What further can be said, about specifically social arrangements?

V.1 The nuclear family has become a problem. In **I.3.2** an argument was made for the extended family. In the last decades, single-person households have proliferated and many children are being raised by one parent.

V.1.1 Therefore: friendship-groups become an alternative to inadequately humane kinship-groups and isolation. Mobility tends to weaken both kinship and friendship bonds. Under such conditions as those summarized in **V** above, more persons will remain home, and the possibilities of cementing friendships and reconstituting extended families will improve.

V.1.2 One parent can raise a child only with difficulty. Since the parent is often the mother, and friendship bonds among women are often likelier to come about than such bonds among men – men being more likely to form bonds based on one or another hierarchical principle rather than on friendship defined in part by equality – several single mothers might choose to pool their resources and live together, forming small voluntary clans devoted to mutual help and childrearing. Mothers can alternate dropping temporarily out of the economy in order to provide continuous presence for the children: many different arrangements become possible. The mother-infant bond would be preserved; daycare would be avoided; and all the mothers would help and be helped.

The multiplication of such maternal clans would be a considerable benefit to society. Pressures would be relieved as often from men as from women.

V.1.3 This is not to say that the nuclear family will disappear. Studies of the adolescent brain – adolescence defined as lasting until one's late twenties – have shown a degree of unavoidable weakness of judgment coupled to weak impulse-control in young women and men. Early marriage should therefore be discouraged. This matter can be taken up in the educational system, relating neuroscience to social questions and giving extended attention to parenting skills.

V.1.4 Later marriages might also look to the social desirability of exogamy: persons of color marrying whites, Christians marrying Muslims, citizens of one country marrying citizens of another country, and so on.

Six

International Relations

VI The challenge is the elimination of war. The first point to be made is that war is not inevitable. We are not programmed for war. In fact human DNA possesses the genetic material for the dampening of hostile impulses. Chimpanzee DNA does not share that genetic material; chimps fight all the time. Bonobo DNA does share it; bonobos do not fight. We need not fight. We can and often enough do get murderously angry, but we need not do murder.

VI.1 We persevere in classic diplomatic work, negotiating arms reduction, doing everything that can be done to prevent nuclear proliferation, resolving disputes of every kind non-violently.

VI.2 We persevere in now classic consensus theory, digging deeper into how cooperation works and into such notions as "symbolic concession," developed by Robert

Axelrod and Scott Atran, and "linking pins," developed by Rensis Likert and Frederick Thayer. Such theories are increasingly useful to the work of diplomacy.

VI.3 Exogamous marriage, mentioned in **V.1.4** in connection with social relations in general, is as pertinent to humane international relations as to humane relations at home. Americans marrying Russians, or American Christians marrying Egyptian Muslims, are examples of peace-preserving exogamy. One nation would be reluctant to wreak havoc on a second nation in which children and grandchildren of the first nation lived.

Seven

Nature

VII A poignant ancillary loss accompanying modernity's loss of clan kinship is our loss of kinship with nature. Even if clan kinship continues to erode, we must reconstitute the human family's kinship with the rest of the natural world.

VII.1 One of the principal matters that will be taken up in the public-school curriculum described in **II.1-9** is totemism. Claude Levi-Strauss called totemism the great mystery of the human condition. Penetration of that mystery will (a) restore our kinship with the natural world, and at the same time (b) elucidate the second sense of "symbol" referred to in **II.6** in connection with plenitude, and (c) contribute to our understanding of a world moving, **VI,** toward the elimination of war.

For many centuries before the coming of the city – in the Middle East five or six thousand years ago – genetically fully modern human beings conducted their external, social lives in kinship clans and their internal, symbol-making lives under the aspect of plenitude. We may call the synthesis of our ancestors' external and internal lives totemism.

A clan member was herself a symbol under the aspect of plenitude. That is to say, she was identified with the other members of her clan; with the origin story of her clan; with a living animal, her clan's totem; and with the carved representation of that animal: she was all those things: *that* is plenitude. She could not marry a member of her own clan; because she was identified with everyone else in the clan, another member of the clan was understood as her as well as himself. She "married out" – exogamy. It was exactly these marriages that insured peaceful relations among clans – hence the appeal to exogamy in **V.1.4** and **VI.3.** Clan society and plenitude seem also to have supplied the setting for the activation of our genetic propensity to dampen anger.

Urban civilization, spreading outward from the Middle East and other centers, weakened or broke clan kinship in favor of urbanism's new hierarchical institutions, and it contracted plenitude into precision. So we were given hierarchical economies, polities, militaries, and religions in place of the authority of kinship elders, and we were given prose literatures and mathematical science in place of a world of persons, things, and processes that collected and communicated a multiplicity of meanings.

Only such a sense of thirty thousand years worldwide can clarify where we are now. We may or may not recover something like clan kinship. Perhaps tax incentives can encourage the reconstitution of extended families in the interests of compassionate childrearing. Perhaps voluntary clans of single mothers will complement traditional clans. Perhaps encouraging the symbolism of plenitude in a superior school system will restore the identifications with nature that were integral to the pre-urban millennia of totemic life. At the very least, we know where to put our energies.

First and Last Things

Svidrigailov in *Crime and Punishment* makes readers cringe. He haunts us, as if he has something to tell us that we need to know but don't want to hear. This is what he dreams on the last night of his life.

He was dozing off; the feverish shiver had ceased, when suddenly something seemed to run over his arm and leg under the bedclothes. He started. "Ugh! hang it! I believe it's a mouse," he thought, "that's the veal I left on the table." He felt fearfully disinclined to pull off the blanket, get up, get cold, but all at once something unpleasant ran over his leg again. He pulled off the blanket and lighted the candle. Shaking with feverish chill he bent down to examine the bed: there was nothing. He shook the blanket and suddenly a mouse jumped out on the sheet. He tried to catch it, but the mouse ran to and fro in zigzags without leaving the bed, slipped between his fingers, ran over his hand and suddenly darted under the pillow. He threw down the pillow, but in one instant felt something leap on his chest and dart over his body and down his back under his shirt. **He trembled nervously and woke up.**

The room was dark. He was lying on the bed and wrapped up in the blanket as before. The wind was howling under the window. "How disgusting," he thought with annoyance.

He got up and sat on the edge of the bedstead with his back to the window. "It's better not to sleep at all," he decided. There was a cold damp draught from the window, however; without getting up he drew the blanket over him and wrapped himself in it. He was not thinking of anything and did not want to think. But one image rose after

another, incoherent scraps of thought without beginning or end
passed through his mind. He sank into drowsiness. Perhaps the cold, or
the dampness, or the dark, or the wind that howled under the window
and tossed the trees roused a sort of persistent craving for the
fantastic. He kept dwelling on images of flowers, he fancied a
charming flower garden, a bright, warm, almost hot day, a holiday-
Trinity day. A fine, sumptuous country cottage in the English taste
overgrown with fragrant flowers, with flower beds going round the
house; the porch, wreathed in climbers, was surrounded with beds of
roses. A light, cool staircase, carpeted with rich rugs, was decorated
with rare plants in china pots. He noticed particularly in the windows
nosegays of tender, white, heavily fragrant narcissus bending over
their bright, green, thick long stalks. He was reluctant to move
away from them, but he went up the stairs and came into a large,
high drawing-room and again everywhere- at the windows, the doors on
to the balcony, and on the balcony itself- were flowers. The floors
were strewn with freshly-cut fragrant hay, the windows were open, a
fresh, cool, light air came into the room. The birds were chirruping
under the window, and in the middle of the room, on a table covered
with a white satin shroud, stood a coffin. The coffin was covered with
white silk and edged with a thick white frill; wreaths of flowers
surrounded it on all sides. Among the flowers lay a girl in a white
muslin dress, with her arms crossed and pressed on her bosom, as
though carved out of marble. But her loose fair hair was wet; there
was a wreath of roses on her head. The stern and already rigid profile
of her face looked as though chiseled of marble too, and the smile on
her pale lips was full of an immense unchildish misery and sorrowful
appeal. Svidrigailov knew that girl; there was no holy image, no
burning candle beside the coffin; no sound of prayers: the girl had
drowned herself. She was only fourteen, but her heart was broken.
And she had destroyed herself, crushed by an insult that had
appalled and amazed that childish soul, had smirched that angel purity
with unmerited disgrace and torn from her a last scream of despair,
unheeded and brutally disregarded, on a dark night in the cold and wet
while the wind howled....

Svidrigailov came to himself, got up from the bed and went to the
window. He felt for the latch and opened it. The wind lashed furiously

into the little room and stung his face and his chest, only covered
with his shirt, as though with frost. Under the window there must have
been something like a garden, and apparently a pleasure garden. There,
too, probably there were tea tables and singing in the daytime. Now
drops of rain flew in at the window from the trees and bushes; it
was dark as in a cellar, so that he could only just make out some dark
blurs of objects. Svidrigailov, bending down with elbows on the
window-sill, gazed for five minutes into the darkness; the boom of a
cannon, followed by a second one, resounded in the darkness of the
night. "Ah, the signal! The river is overflowing," he thought. "By
morning it will be swirling down the street in the lower parts,
flooding the basements and cellars. The cellar rats will swim out, and
men will curse in the rain and wind as they drag their rubbish to
their upper storeys. What time is it now?" And he had hardly thought
it when, somewhere near, a clock on the wall, ticking away
hurriedly, struck three.

  "Aha! It will be light in an hour! Why wait? I'll go out at once
straight to the park. I'll choose a great bush there drenched with
rain, so that as soon as one's shoulder touches it, millions of
drops drip on one's head."

  He moved away from the window, shut it, lighted the candle, put on
his waistcoat, his overcoat and his hat and went out, carrying the
candle, into the passage to look for the ragged attendant who would be
asleep somewhere in the midst of candle ends and all sorts of rubbish,
to pay him for the room and leave the hotel. "It's the best minute;
I couldn't choose a better."

  He walked for some time through a long narrow corridor without
finding any one and was just going to call out, when suddenly in a
dark corner between an old cupboard and the door he caught sight of
a strange object which seemed to be alive. He bent down with the
candle and saw a little girl, not more than five years old,
shivering and crying, with her clothes as wet as a soaking
house-flannel. She did not seem afraid of Svidrigailov, but looked
at him with blank amazement out of her big black eyes. Now and then
she sobbed as children do when they have been crying a long time,
but are beginning to be comforted. The child's face was pale and
tired, she was numb with cold. "How can she have come here? She must

have hidden here and not slept all night." He began questioning her.
The child suddenly becoming animated, chattered away in her baby
language, something about "mammy" and that "mammy would beat her," and
about some cup that she had "bwoken." The child chattered on without
stopping. He could only guess from what she said that she was a
neglected child, whose mother, probably a drunken cook, in the service
of the hotel, whipped and frightened her; that the child had broken
a cup of her mother's and was so frightened that she had run away
the evening before, had hidden for a long while somewhere outside in
the rain, at last had made her way in here, hidden behind the cupboard
and spent the night there, crying and trembling from the damp, the
darkness and the fear that she would be badly beaten for it. He took
her in his arms, went back to his room, sat her on the bed, and
began undressing her. The torn shoes which she had on her stockingless
feet were as wet as if they had been standing in a puddle all night.
When he had undressed her, he put her on the bed, covered her up and
wrapped her in the blanket from her head downwards. She fell asleep at
once. Then he sank into dreary musing again.

 "What folly to trouble myself," he decided suddenly with an
oppressive feeling of annoyance. "What idiocy!" In vexation he took up
the candle to go and look for the ragged attendant again and make
haste to go away. "Damn the child!" he thought as he opened the
door, but he turned again to see whether the child was asleep. He
raised the blanket carefully. The child was sleeping soundly, she
had got warm under the blanket, and her pale cheeks were flushed.
But strange to say that flush seemed brighter and coarser than the
rosy cheeks of childhood. "It's a flush of fever," thought
Svidrigailov. It was like the flush from drinking, as though she had
been given a full glass to drink. Her crimson lips were hot and
glowing; but what was this? He suddenly fancied that her long black
eyelashes were quivering, as though the lids were opening and a sly
crafty eye peeped out with an unchildlike wink, as though the little
girl were not asleep, but pretending. Yes, it was so. Her lips
parted in a smile. The corners of her mouth quivered, as though she
were trying to control them. But now she quite gave up all effort, now
it was a grin, a broad grin; there was something shameless,
provocative in that quite unchildish face; it was depravity, it was

the face of a harlot, the shameless face of a French harlot. Now
both eyes opened wide; they turned a glowing, shameless glance upon
him; they laughed, invited him.... There was something infinitely
hideous and shocking in that laugh, in those eyes, in such nastiness
in the face of a child. "What, at five years old?" Svidrigailov
muttered in genuine horror. "What does it mean?" And now she turned to
him, her little face all aglow, holding out her arms.... "Accursed
child!" Svidrigailov cried, raising his hand to strike her, but **at
that moment he woke up**.

He was in the same bed, still wrapped in the blanket. The candle had
not been lighted, and daylight was streaming in at the windows.

"I've had nightmare all night!" He got up angrily, feeling utterly
shattered; his bones ached. There was a thick mist outside and he
could see nothing. It was nearly five. He had overslept himself! He
got up, put on his still damp jacket and overcoat. Feeling the
revolver in his pocket, he took it out and then he sat down, took a
notebook out of his pocket and in the most conspicuous place on the
title page wrote a few lines in large letters. Reading them over, he
sank into thought with his elbows on the table. The revolver and the
notebook lay beside him. Some flies woke up and settled on the
untouched veal, which was still on the table. He stared at them and at
last with his free right hand began trying to catch one. He tried till
he was tired, but could not catch it. At last, realising that he was
engaged in this interesting pursuit, he started, got up and walked
resolutely out of the room. A minute later he was in the street.

A thick milky mist hung over the town. Svidrigailov walked along the
slippery dirty wooden pavement towards the Little Neva. He was
picturing the waters of the Little Neva swollen in the night,
Petrovsky Island, the wet paths, the wet grass, the wet trees and
bushes and at last the bush.... He began ill-humouredly staring at the
houses, trying to think of something else. There was not a cabman or a
passer-by in the street. The bright yellow, wooden, little houses
looked dirty and dejected with their closed shutters. The cold and
damp penetrated his whole body and he began to shiver. From time to
time he came across shop signs and read each carefully. At last he
reached the end of the wooden pavement and came to a big stone
house. A dirty, shivering dog crossed his path with its tail between

its legs. A man in a great coat lay face downwards; dead drunk, across the pavement. He looked at him and went on. A high tower stood up on the left. "Bah!" he shouted, "here is a place. Why should it be Petrovsky? It will be in the presence of an official witness anyway...."

He almost smiled at this new thought and turned into the street where there was the big house with the tower. At the great closed gates of the house, a little man stood with his shoulder leaning against them, wrapped in a grey soldier's coat, with a copper Achilles helmet on his head. He cast a drowsy and indifferent glance at Svidrigailov. His face wore that perpetual look of peevish dejection, which is so sourly printed on all faces of Jewish race without exception. They both, Svidrigailov and Achilles, stared at each other for a few minutes without speaking. At last it struck Achilles as irregular for a man not drunk to be standing three steps from him, staring and not saying a word.

"What do you want here?" he said, without moving or changing his position.

"Nothing, brother, good morning," answered Svidrigailov.

"This isn't the place."

"I am going to foreign parts, brother."

"To foreign parts?"

"To America."

"America."

Svidrigailov took out the revolver and cocked it. Achilles raised his eyebrows.

"I say, this is not the place for such jokes!"

"Why shouldn't it be the place?"

"Because it isn't."

"Well, brother, I don't mind that. It's a good place. When you are asked, you just say he was going, he said, to America."

He put the revolver to his right temple.

"You can't do it here, it's not the place," cried Achilles, rousing himself, his eyes growing bigger and bigger.

Svidrigailov pulled the trigger.

Constance Garnett's translation

I've boldfaced both awakenings. Svidrigailov may have dreamt twice in the ordinary way, but I think he dreamt only once. I read this passage as describing a dream within a dream, as if what Freud was to call the unconscious system has an unconscious subsystem of its own. From the images of the framing dream and those of the embedded dream we can only conclude that the farther down into the overall unconscious we go, the more horrifying things become. An ultimate horror, then, must lie at the deepest layer of the psyche, at the foundation of the human condition.

The notion that the psyche, if not the unconscious system, is layered appears in *The Interpretation of Dreams,* written thirty-three years after *Crime and Punishment.* The divide is between the conscious and unconscious systems. Freud's account of the dynamisms of the unconscious system has inspired an enormous literature, by turns admiring, amplificatory, critical, and hostile, and always heated: the stakes are always high, since the question is, Who are we?

Ignacio Matte-Blanco is a Chilean psychoanalyst. He accepts Freud's hypothesis that unconscious processes not only exist but are primary determinants both of dream- and waking life, and he goes on to accept Dostoyevsky's suggestion that *levels* of unconscious processes exist and work their way with us. But Matte-Blanco doesn't find what either Freud or Dostoyevsky found at the first, deepest level of mental life. His practice presented him with a five-tiered stratigraphy of the psyche:

Tier 1, characterized by asymmetry, heterogeneity, numeracy, and exactitude regarding commonsense time and space. "Asymmetry" means, for example, that Margaret is Elizabeth's daughter, so Elizabeth cannot be Margaret's daughter.

Tier 2, characterized by the introduction of emotion, of the simile "is like" if not the metaphor "is," and by the first intrusion of symmetry. "Symmetry" means that we can begin to contemplate that Margaret being Elizabeth's daughter and Elizabeth being Margaret's daughter might both be true.

Tier 3, characterized by the introduction of the intended metaphor A is in fact B, and by a degree of timelessness and spacelessness.

Tier 4, characterized by considerable symmetry and the denial of Aristotelian non-contradiction. This is Freud's unconscious system.

Tier 5, characterized by symmetry, homogeneity, non-numeracy, timelessness, and spacelessness, where the "endless number of things…become, mysteriously, only one thing." Its mode is neither simile nor metaphor, but synechdoche, by which any part of a whole is the whole. Tier 5 is the base layer of human consciousness, where "we all experience a unity between ourselves and everybody and everything else." While the principle of "divisibility" operates at Tier 1, that of "indivisibility" operates at Tier 5. [Ignacio Matte-Blanco, *Thinking, Feeling, and Being,* London, Routledge, 1988; 27ff. The method by which Matte-Blanco arrives at his characterizations is fully developed in *The Unconscious as Infinite Sets,* London, Duckworth, 1975.]

Two foundations of mental life, one violent, implying little hope for the human future, the other peaceful, requiring no anxiety about the human future. An interesting school of anthropologically informed linguistics appears to favor the latter foundation over the former. "First peoples" are fast disappearing, rendering an appeal to a human group that has never submitted to urbanization almost impossible; still, Daniel Everett, a linguist, has reached an astonishing conclusion about one such group, living deep in the Amazon rainforest.

According to Everett, the language spoken by this group, the Piraha, doesn't have at its foundation what the regnant school of linguistics insists it must have, recursion. Recursion is preeminently a feature of Matte-Blanco's Tier 1. It's the foundation of Aristotle's Organon, for the West after the fourth century B.C. the rulebook of thinking itself. The unexamined axioms of the Organon are, first, that words have one and only one meaning, and, two, that groups of words correctly strung together can be fit into other correctly strung-together groups of words in the same way sets can be inserted into larger sets as subsets. I'll return to the first axiom. As to the second, the axiom of recursion: it doesn't ground the Piraha language. Here is a first people who live closer to Tier 5 than to Tier 1. They're radical presentists, paying no attention either to the past or the future; they eschew counting; and they're cheerful. When I take up the single meanings of words, I'll also add singing to the repertoire of Piraha daily life. [Daniel L. Everett, *Don't Sleep, There Are Snakes,* NY, Random House, 2008.]

The following argument will let me tie Dostoyevsky, Freud, Matte-Blanco, and Everett to Schopenhauer and my conclusions about words, music, and first and last things. The argument is a revised excerpt from my *Prolegomena to Any Future History,* and it incidentally supplies definitions for the terminology you'll encounter in the schematic introduction to the next essay in this volume.

Differentiation and de-differentiation

We awake to a world of perceptually differentiated entities. We may proceed conceptually in that world in two ways. We may continue to differentiate in the world or part of the world: we make a cut or draw a distinction in an empty field in order to differentiate one region in the field from another region in it. Or we may de-differentiate in the world or part of the world: we erase or heal over a cut in a field, undoing a distinction in it.

For purposes of taking a botany examination, for example, one might take the field "trees" and differentiate deciduous from evergreen trees, then continue in the same vein by differentiating evergreen pines from evergreen spruces, and then evergreen white pines from evergreen red pines. For purposes of enlarging social justice in a society, on the other hand, one might take the field of male, black, and white adults and ignore every perceptually given differentiation: de-differentiating for gender, yielding all black and white adults; de-differentiating for color, yielding all adults; and de-differentiating for age, yielding all persons.

Each mental operation, differentiation and de-differentiation, carries with it a constellation of structures and performances. The constellation generated by differentiation first.

Constituting a world under the aspect of differentiation

When we differentiate exclusively, we construct a world of very many separate and distinct entities, substantially different from one another. Let us call that kind of world *plurisubstantial.* A plurisubstantial world tends to acquire a hierarchical structure. Hierarchies generally reveal a top stratum with little room on it, a bottom stratum with a good deal of room, and a number of strata in between. Large hierarchical corporations, for example, will have a few upper managers, a larger number of middle managers, and many more non-managerial employees. Armies similarly. Power and rewards concentrate at the top of such hierarchies and thin out as one goes down them. CEOs and generals make more important decisions than cost-accountants and captains, tell cost-accountants and captains what to do, and get paid more than cost-accountants and captains. One stratum of the hierarchy taken by itself will be differentiated with an exactitude proportional to the intensity of the differentiating activity that produced the hierarchy. Especially intense differentiation produced the modern world's armies, and military strata are finely cross-hatched into job-descriptions. A hierarchy taken three-dimensionally, then, is a tiered pyramid the strata of which represent differences in status, power, and reward within the hierarchy, the compartments on each stratum representing different functions at the same level of status, power, and reward.

Hierarchies like corporations and armies are whole societies. The "parts" of those wholes are the employees and soldiers in service to the hierarchies. Is there something that can be said about employees and soldiers that can be generalized to any parts of any hierarchical whole? It seems that as any hierarchy becomes more and more articulated vertically and horizontally, more plurisubstantial, the parts of the hierarchy contract; they empty in content, tending toward single meanings or ***univocity.***

Contraction is synonymous with emptying because less and less of an employee's or soldier's repertory of competencies and interests as a complete human being will be exercised at work or in the field. This emptying while hierarchized carries over to the person's life away from work or the military. She will be pained that so much has been taken, abstracted, from her. So her life is comprehensively emptier as a result of her enterprise's success.

Added to her abstraction – in several senses of "abstraction" – is division. Many employees in the middle of a corporate hierarchy are obliged both to follow orders and to give them. This is obviously the case in the military. The same person may act obsequiously one moment looking up a stratum in the hierarchy and arrogantly the next moment looking down a stratum. She may not realize that she acts in these ways, or she may give such behaviors other, more acceptable names. Nonetheless, for half or more of their waking lives during the week, many corporate employees live reduced, abstract and abstracted, disturbingly divided lives as emptying parts of hierarchical wholes, a condition that darkens the remaining hours of their week.

Differentiation, plurisubstantiality, hierarchy, univocity.

Speaking a world under the aspect of differentiation

One of the privileged wholes in the human world is surely language. We humans never stop talking. We discover or confirm worlds with words. If differentiation creates plurisubstantial, hierarchical wholes and abstract, emptying parts, then we will expect that linguistic wholes in the realm of differentiation will be plurisubstantial and hierarchical, and linguistic parts will be abstract and near-empty. The parts of social hierarchies are people. The parts of linguistic hierarchies are words. People empty out in social hierarchies; words empty out in linguistic hierarchies.

Languages created by persistence-in-differentiation can be viewed as vertically stratified and horizontally cross-hatched as follows:

the word: a univocal semantic

small word-groups: an ordered syntactic

larger word-groups: a strongly ordered logistic

extensive traditions of word-groups: hypotaxis

The word taken by itself sits at the top of this hierarchy. It is abstract and emptying, a classic part-of-a-hierarchical-whole. Its principal feature will decide questions on every lower level of the linguistic hierarchy. That feature is univocity, the abstraction of all the word's meanings but one.

Most of us do not use words all by themselves. We group them into sentences or sentence-like clusters. At this second level of the linguistic hierarchy, we are told, meaning comes as much from the relationships among words as from the words themselves. Asymmetric orderliness becomes a preoccupation. In languages like English, the sequence subject-predicate-object becomes a model of asymmetric orderliness.

Assume that our words are univocal and our small-scale ordering, our syntax, passes all tests for order. The next-stratum-down in the hierarchy carries groups of small-scale word-groups. There are many ways to group together small-scale word-groups like sentences: into spoken conversations, into letters home, into novels, poems. We will look at a severe and particularly consequential grouping principle, the one that creates logistic.

The second, syntactic level of the linguistic hierarchy *often* displays a three-part, subject-predicate-object order. On the third, logistic level of the hierarchy, we *always* find a three-part order – never an elegant variation – this time of

   1) universal statement(s)
   2) particular statement(s)
   3) conclusion

Each of these statements possesses its own subject-predicate-object structure. Each subject, predicate, and object will in turn be univocal. All hierarchical relations are preserved.

Universals are statements claiming to be true in any place and at any time. Particulars are statements claiming to be true in one place at one time. Conclusions are particular statements – true in one place at one time – that are entailed by properly selected universals and particulars. The full set, universal-particular-conclusion, can be called a law. Two kinds of laws interest us:

   social laws, with which civilized societies will be put together,
   and
   scientific laws, toward the discovery of which civilized inquiry will be conducted.

The first formal social laws appeared in Sumer, off the Persian Gulf, about fifty-five hundred years ago. They are of the form,

   1) any person doing that thing, in any place and at any time, is guilty of a
        crime and will be punished in this prescribed way
   2) that person over there, in that place and at this time, is doing exactly
        that thing

3) that person over there is guilty of that crime, and will be punished in
    this prescribed way

The first formal scientific laws appeared in Greece about twenty-five hundred years ago. A philosopher of science has described scientific laws in a story. A car is left on the street on a very cold night. Its radiator is filled with water. The particular statements in the story include these facts, plus the exact temperature and air pressure outside. The universal statements in the story include the freezing temperature of water, the rate at which water pressure increases, and the bursting pressure of the radiator metal. The conclusion of the story is that the radiator cracked. It had no choice but to crack. The entire three-part deduction is the "explanation" of the cracked radiator.

Such a deduction leads to prediction as well as explanation. If the night in question were tonight – a freezing midwinter night and we have a reliable weather forecast assuring us of an equally cold morning – then we would know right now what the condition of the radiator will be tomorrow. We would have predicted the future. The univocal logistic seeks prediction and its conviction of control over the future. We will soon discover a painful anxiety attached to the future in worlds built by persistence-in-differentiation.

Observe that the form of social laws, which, we must remember, are also concerned with prediction and control, is exactly the same as the form of scientific laws. This form becomes a foundation-layer of both the internal and external lives of the modern world. Let us call the third, logistic stratum of the univocal linguistic hierarchy "the curriculum of civilization."

The fourth level of the linguistic hierarchy includes longer and longer word-spans, like books and literary traditions. A general characterization of the base level of the hierarchy will be useful in comparing differentiated worlds to de-differentiated worlds. The base is "hypotactic," a term that suggests "arranged hierarchically," and "showing subordinations." We see hypotactic structures in all hierarchized places, not only in literary traditions. A life can be regarded or lived hypotactically: everything arranged, every arrangement the best arrangement possible, each arrangement following the last in the correct order.

There are two deep-lying hypotactic structures in most of our lives that are almost never construed as hypotactic; they are understood simply as givens, as the way things are and always have been. For that reason they need to be illuminated with special care. They are not "the way things are," but the way they are under the aegis of differentiation.

The first of these hypotaxes is space, visual and aural. People who live in largely differentiated worlds see and hear hierarchically. That is to say, they see and hear only some elements of a visual or aural space, those elements that they (often instantaneously, perhaps unconsciously) think are important to see and hear. They barely see or hear the other, hypotactically subordinated elements in their spaces. The Gestalt psychologists of the 1930's might have said that they see and hear "foregrounds"; the rest they push into "backgrounds." With persistence in differentiation, foregrounds shrink, leaving enlarged backgrounds. Recall that (1) persons empty to single functions in hierarchical organizations and (2) words empty to single meanings in hierarchical languages. Here we see that (3) perceptual spaces can also empty, to smaller and smaller foregrounds.

The second hypotaxis, time, is a much more complex problem, more hidden, more taken for granted as unproblematical, and, if anything, more important to understanding modernity and ourselves. Time is more perfectly hypotactic in the differentiated world than is any particular tradition in words, tones, stone, pigment, or social, political, or economic arrangements. Perhaps time is a privileged category and it must be made unequivocally hypotactic before any other more-or-less hypotactic tradition can emerge.

Picture a time-line with a point at its center signifying the present. We now invoke "the curriculum of civilization": universal statements apply everywhere on the time-line; particular statements make up a chronicle to the left of the present, the past. Among the particulars,

> some are causes; effects fall to their right on the line
>
> some are means; ends fall to their right on the line
>
> some are particular statements in laws; conclusions fall to their right on the line

A past is now revealed that carries complete causal, means-ends, and lawful structures.

Next, take an enlarged cut at the present. This moment reveals *in*complete structures. There are causes, means, and particular statements in it without effects, ends, or conclusions for them. We need a place, a future, to accommodate those effects, ends, and conclusions. So we go ahead and create a future. Its role is to provide the one and only one place where incomplete hypotactic structures can be completed. This future must be articulated in exactly the same way that the past, the site holding complete hypotactic structures, is itself articulated. Before long, after all, the immediate future will be the immediate past.

Hypotactic time has a specific intellectual tone. Interest in causal, means-ends, and lawful relationships places a modern person's attention in the past, from which he or she "learns," that is, becomes at ease with complete hypotactic structures, and in the future, into which he or she "plans," that is, projects the completing elements of incomplete present structures. Learning from the past and planning for the future become highly valued ways to use the mind in such differentiating, distinction-making, univocal cultures as our own.

The emotional tone of hypotactic time is another matter. Preoccupations with effects, ends, and conclusions, preoccupations with prediction and control, create culture-wide preoccupations with the future. The problem for emotional life is that a fixation on the future cannot help but lead to a fixation on personal death. One's death has not happened in the past and it is not happening as one speaks; it can only happen in the future. Unfortunately, the more futurity, the more death-haunted the present.

Acting in a world under the aspect of differentiation

Thinking about the textures of living and dying takes us to questions of action. Of course, speaking is already acting, since so many human connections and disconnections are made with words. We speak ourselves into love and hate, into cooperation and competition, into every degree of attraction and repulsion. We naturally ask whether certain kinds of speaking are more likely to have particular personal and social consequences than other kinds.

The curriculum of civilization helps us to answer that question. Learning to excel in the curriculum, in the logistic, is often to acquire a skill that finds its possessor pitted against others possessing the skill in other degrees. These engagements of the logistically equipped generally become unequal-outcome contests: the better-equipped contestant wins, the less-well-equipped contestant loses.

There are three unequal-outcome-contest patterns, the classic zero-sum pattern and the unequal-outcome negative-sum and unequal-outcome positive-sum patterns. The latter two are to be distinguished from *equal*-outcome negative-sum and equal-outcome positive-sum patterns. The equal-outcome patterns do not yield contests. Any tendency in the sphere of action for two persons or groups of persons to enter into unequal-outcome contests will hierarchize those persons. The winners will rise, the losers fall. They will all adopt the emptying and divided personality-structure characteristic of hierarchized persons. Where the hierarchy restricts room at the top by multiplying contests, the pyramid with which we are familiar will take shape.

The pyramid we saw in "constituting a world…" is in the minds of individual differentiators. It is the internal plan for world-making when the mind is used principally to differentiate fields of perception and experience. The pyramid we now see, in "acting in a world…," is a social pyramid. Does the micro-hierarchy in the mind create the macro-hierarchy in society? Does the way we think determine the way we live, or does it work the other way? Because we live in social hierarchies, do we project that social reality back into the mind and make or "find" thinking hierarchical? It does not matter to us just now where this circle begins. What matters is to recognize how powerful a circle it is, joining the most intangible, private, mental processes, through spoken and written words, which are both private and public, to the most tangible, public, social processes.

There exists a second circle, equally seamless and consistent, generated by actively de-differentiating the perceptually differentiated world. Differentiated worlds, demarcated both vertically in levels or strata or floors of a high-rise corporate headquarters, and horizontally in job-descriptions of one sort or another, are worlds made up of many separate things of many different kinds. The boundaries separating one kind from another are impermeable. A tree is only a tree, never a tree and a bird; a bird is only a bird, never a bird and a tree.

Constituting a world under the aspect of de-differentiation

If we were to imagine those boundaries thinner, like the bi-directional, semi-permeable membranes of living cells, then under special conditions certain entities could pass through the boundaries or membranes and fuse with each other, making a ***polysemy.*** Sometimes a tree *could* be a tree and a bird. A person could be a person and a tree and a bird. The world in which that polysemous person lived would not always be plurisubstantial; there would be occasions when her world was something like a single substance, nearly boundary-free. Let us call such a world, much less demarcated either vertically or horizontally than the plurisubstantial world, ***unisubstantial.*** Parts of de-differentiated, unisubstantial wholes can fill; they are "concrete," in contrast to the emptying, abstract parts of differentiated, plurisubstantial wholes.

De-differentiation, unisubstantiality, non-hierarchy, polysemy.

Speaking a world under the aspect of de-differentiation

We come to the languages of de-differentiation. They can be viewed as follows:

the word: a polysemous semantic

small word-groups: a barely ordered syntactic

larger word-groups: a virtually absent logistic

extensive traditions of word-groups: parataxis

The word taken by itself in the differentiated, univocal linguistic hierarchy is important; its precision is necessary for syntax to proceed correctly. Precise words and correct syntax are necessary for the logistic to lock tight. The payoff is the logistic. That is where the cultural weight lies in differentiating languages. That is where social laws are made and natural laws are made or discovered.

The word taken by itself in the de-differentiated, polysemous linguistic *non*-hierarchy is even more important. Almost all the weight in de-differentiating languages lies with the word. There is little weight on the barely existing syntactic and logistic strata. That is why it is appropriate to say that there is no hierarchy here, and no "curriculum."

One might wonder why words count for more than word-groups in a polysemous language. The positive reason is immediately apparent: full words communicate a great deal. They are like the full persons we can now begin to understand, and like the full moments we will soon encounter in paratactic time. The negative reasons are less apparent. They shed additional light on univocal syntax and the univocal logistic.

When in a univocal language you carry the precise word down to a correctly formed sentence and then carry the sentence down to a correctly formed law, all those words must maintain their meanings while in transit in the linguistic hierarchy. You can not tolerate a noun like "person" in a level-two sentence changing its meaning to "person-tree" in one statement in a level-three law and to "person-tree-bird" in another statement at level three, and then expect that the law will work properly. A person (level one) must be a person (level two) must be a person (level three). Such constancy is a requirement of univocity.

Polysemous nouns, on the other hand, can expand or contract in meaning between levels. That precludes the levels from crystallizing. So the weight of meaning in a de-differentiating language stays right at the top with the word by itself. First, it belongs there; second, it can not be anywhere else.

When words, not as word-groups but just as words, are considered collectively, they may be thought to constitute "parataxis." While hypotaxis denotes orderliness, parataxis denotes non-orderliness. Parataxis suggests coordination more than subordination, and any number of sequences rather than a single correct sequence. Parataxis de-hierarchizes the world. The filling parts of paratactic, unisubstantial wholes never array themselves hierarchically, but exist in a flat, coordinate, non-order.

Parataxis is concerned with the concrete thing itself, the local and contained, and the moment, rather than with relationships among abstract things and over-arching spatial and temporal schemes. Paratactic stories, often the favorites of children, include numbers of exciting episodes with little or no relation to each other. They can be put in any order, and begun anywhere. It is not unusual for teachers of adult literature to proclaim an evolution from such "primitive" parataxis to an ever more "civilized" hypotaxis. It is upsetting to some teachers to find Ernest Hemingway, who removes hierarchizing conjunctions from his sentences, arriving on the scene after Henry James. Teachers of ancient history, similarly, may move quickly through Egypt, where the texts are not hypotactic, so that they can spend more time with Greece, which practically re-invents hypotaxis. And surely the most famous un-read book of our time is *Finnegans Wake*, which places itself squarely in a polysemous linguistic world. There may be no literary work that makes univocal readers more anxious. So runs the opposition of parataxis and hypotaxis: lumpish piles, but of extraordinary things, against extraordinary structures, but of near-empty things.

Paratactic space and paratactic time make dramatic antitheses to their hypotactic counterparts. Vision supplies plentiful examples of the two kinds of perception. A person looking ahead of him on a forest path, looking hypotactically because he spends most of his time in the differentiating mode, will see what is important to him – birds, if he is a bird-watcher. Another person, walking down the same path but seeing paratactically, will see much more than the first person. The second person's space will be fuller of things. The phenomenon of paratactic persons taking in more of the world, living in a fuller world, than hypotactic persons, has been reported time and time again by (hypotactic) travelers among (paratactic) traditional peoples.

The case of paratactic time appears more obscure than that of paratactic space, as we might expect, and it is critical to understanding human prospects. Hypotactic time took what space it did to describe because it was necessary to bring the curriculum of civilization to bear on it. We needed to follow the construction of the future from nothing so that it might receive effects, ends, and conclusions. But there is no curriculum in the polysemous linguistic world.

In paratactic time there is little past because there are no complete logistic structures to be sought there, and there is little future because there is no need for a place in which to complete incomplete logistic structures. There is certainly a present, gathering to itself much of the energy that hypotactic persons give to the past and future, and inhabited by full persons and full objects: a full present. The present of hypotactic time often enough takes third place behind the past and the future, depleted of energy: an empty present.

We would expect to find the emotional tone associated with paratactic time quite different from the emotional tone associated with hypotactic time. A person living in paratactic time can not be anxiety-ridden about the future, there being little of futurity in her temporal sense-of-things. There can consequently be little serious anxiety about her death. Because of the insubstantiality of the future and the density and sufficiency of the present, thoughts of personal death, when they do come, are less likely to be characterized by the dread with which they are charged in largely hypotactic cultures. Death-terrors do not inform largely paratactic cultures.

Acting in a world under the aspect of de-differentiation

To ask what does inform a society inclined to parataxis takes us again to action. Contest, which, with its supporting institutions, often infuses societies inclined to hypotaxis, depends greatly on the univocal logistic. That logistic is absent in de-differentiating languages and communities. Just as we saw the future fully present in the differentiation constellation and barely present in the de-differentiation constellation, contest always thrives in the former and hardly exists in the latter. Where there is no weaponry – and logistically wielded word-groups are pre-eminent weapons in contests – it is difficult to fight a war.

In order to learn what social principle animates de-differentiating worlds, we need only remember where the burden of meaning rests in de-differentiating languages. The place is the word alone, and what permits the word to become a polysemy is the power of the imagination to fuse things with one another. Fusion is also the social engine of predominantly paratactic communities. It is the end of action and the means, both.

Fusion may be seen as the opposite of contest. In a community in which fusion is the social aim, children, women, and men thinking and feeling polysemously "become" each other. They already become entities in nature in order to multiply their attributes; they now become each other, in order to constitute a human society.

A non-hierarchical society of full persons closes a circle with the non-hierarchical wholes and concrete parts with which our development of the de-differentiation constellation began. Both of our two circles close on themselves.

Totemism

Univocal and polysemous processes never appear alone, unalloyed. People and communities are mixed. The oldest and most long-lived mixture of the differentiation and de-differentiation constellations is *totemism*. Picture a square field divided vertically into four columns. At the head of each column is a different animal, let us say. Beneath each animal are arrayed the spoken name of the animal, a small amulet in the shape of the animal, an individual person fused to the animal, the entire animal's human clan fused to the animal, and the origin story of the that clan.

Each vertical section of the totemism picture contains animals, names, amulets, individual persons, clans, and stories that are unisubstantial for each other. Helping the animal helps the person; telling the origin story wrong hurts the clan and the animal. Across the picture, though, impermeable boundaries separate the columns. A coyote girl is different from a blacksnake boy. Exogamy, the rule of marriage that preserves inter-clan peace, depends on that difference. A coyote girl can marry a blacksnake boy; she can not marry a coyote boy – can not because they are the same person.

This picture of four vertical columns can be distinguished in one direction from an absolutely empty field, the ideal type of the never encountered, wholly unisubstantial field, and in the other direction from a field cut not only vertically but horizontally as well, erecting walls among all animals, names, amulets, persons, clans, and stories – the now-everywhere encountered plurisubstantial field. Totemism can thus be seen as the middle between unisubstantiality and plurisubstantiality, vertically unisubstantial and horizontally plurisubstantial. It binds persons to other persons so as to multiply personal substance and maintain social amity, and it binds communities to nature to the same ends. It is the world-picture of what can be called *equilibrium kinship*. Perhaps no human arrangement has worked so well, for so long, over so much of the planet.

On history

The decisive moment in hypotactic time, for the human community and indeed for life on earth, is the half-millennium or so between five and six thousand years ago.

"Mixture" will serve as a first historical hypothesis. For the long stretch of time between the genetic consolidation of *homo sapiens sapiens* as the only human occupier of the planet around thirty-five thousand or forty thousand years ago to five or six thousand years ago, more-or-less world-wide, the differentiation and de-differentiation constellations were intermingled. Implied in the mixture hypothesis is the notion of "proximity." Univocal and polysemous processes were "close" to each other. People easily moved between the two constellations. When a serious problem arose, a person or community tended to shift to the univocal constellation. The ocean tide may have been rising unusually quickly around a Pacific island, and the equilibrium-kinship clans there needed to make a plan to protect themselves. The univocal logistic is made to solve problems, so the logistic was activated. When those same people were safe – the condition they tried to live in most of the time – they were more likely to invoke polysemous competencies than univocal ones, since polysemy brought them such pleasure and fellow-feeling.

Danger seems to call up univocity, safety polysemy. It is important to keep this possibility in mind, since a community that wishes to cultivate univocity may choose to increase danger in its own midst, a choice that might appear paradoxical. Such a community might in the same spirit multiply its problems, in so doing stimulating its problem-solving activity, and with it the entire differentiation constellation. If a community wants to stay univocal, nothing helps it do so more than dangers and problems.

In time around fifty-five hundred years ago and in space at the northwestern end of the Persian Gulf,

> mixture was displaced by sorting
>
> and
>
> proximity was displaced by distance

As far as we know, at that time and in that place, univocal processes were first separated out of the millennia-old mixture, to be reinforced by institutions new to the planet – writing systems supported by the first dictionaries, for example; univocal schools; logistical law codes; hierarchical cultural, social, political, and economic aggregates of many kinds. Polysemous processes were correspondingly disconfirmed by those institutions. *Both* univocal and polysemous performances would be weakened in process, since a fully human univocity requires the fusions of polysemy to guide it, and a fully human polysemy requires the instrumental competencies of univocity to bring its aims to fruition. A considerable gap opened between now weak but dominant univocal competencies and weak, suppressed polysemous competencies. This separation would characterize the genus civilization. The different species of civilization would be distinguished by different degrees of separation between the differentiation and de-differentiation constellations.

The significance of the origin of civilization in the Middle East for internal life is that strong differentiating and de-differentiating competencies, which had been mixed and proximate for about thirty-five thousand years, were now being sorted and distanced from each other, recently extracted, weakened differentiating competencies ascending in importance, recently extracted, weakened de-differentiating competencies descending in importance. The significance of the origin of civilization for external life is that social relationships that had been controlled by equilibrium-kinship conventions for about thirty-five thousand years were now being re-ordered into anti-kinship, bureaucratic and hierarchical conventions. Equilibrium kinship would everywhere on earth be replaced by one or another species of civilization. The history of the last fifty-five hundred years has been the story of that replacement, of what has been lost and what has been gained in this or that place, at this or that time.

. . . .

I've referred (1) to a first order of mentation, variously describable as unisubstantial and as showing features of Matte-Blanco's Tier 5, (2) to a first people, the Piraha, whose language reveals the contingent, cultural origin of recursion, and now (3) to a first poetry, polysemy, which, offending Aristotle, asks for multiple rather than single meanings in the word. It remains to look to music.

Few philosophers in the Western philosophical canon take up music. Arthur Schopenhauer not only takes it up, but elevates it over philosophy, claiming that music moves us closest to the first order of reality, the noumenon. Schopenhauer's noumenon is *the* realm of indivisibility, one and undifferentiated. The phenomenal world of differentiated people, chairs, stars, ideas is a second order of reality, of "representations." We phenomena, human amalgams of the noumenon and our parochial equipment for knowing anything at all, cannot know the noumenon pure, on principle, but we can approach it. And no one, nothing, brings us closer to the noumenon than Bach, Mozart, Brahms…. [Arthur Schopenhauer, *The World as Will and Representation,* vol. 1, trans. E.F.J. Payne, NY, Dover Publications, Inc., 1969; pp. 256-7, 260, 262-3.]

What can stand as a *first* music? Should a first music somehow call up unisubstantiality in the psyche, indivisibility in the "universe" – a problematic notion, that of the universe, if you take Kant and Schopenhauer seriously – a first people, a first poetry? Why should a first music come last in such a list? It needs to come last because it's only a first music that can help us look at the last thing that ultimately enlists everybody's interest, and not merely interest, death.

In 2007 John Colapinto wrote a piece for the *The New Yorker* about Everett and the Piraha. Everett's important book is more filled out than the Colapinto piece, but there's a point made at the end of the piece that's not in the book, where Colapinto turns from Everett to his former wife Keren. She tells Colapinto that the single key to learning the Piraha language lies in their singing. By the time this remarkable insight was communicated to Everett, he was impatient to leave the Amazon and get back to Academia. He didn't pursue song. If there's a first people remaining on the planet, the Piraha are it; if there's a first music, it's theirs. [John Colapinto, "A Reporter at Large: The Interpreter," *The New Yorker,* April 16, 2007.]

It's hard for us at the beginning of our lives to go to sleep. There's something deeply troubling about moving from consciousness to the absence of consciousness. Fortunately Piraha parents and our parents have a way to help Piraha children and us go to sleep: they sing. The lullaby is the bridge, perhaps even the universal bridge, from presence to absence of consciousness. I think that there's a privileged lullaby among lullabies – a first lullaby. Like a realm of indivisibility and like polysemy, the first lullaby shows no divisions into particular intervals, let alone words, yet it means everything. It means that the motherly person sitting beside you loves you and you're safe; you can go to sleep. The first lullaby is the meandering, loving *hum.* Like sleep, death is a transition from presence to absence of consciousness. It's the addendum about the next morning that scares us so much. For that reason no one needs the first lullaby more than people at the end of their lives.

Like many bookish people, I've collected "masters of those who know" most of my life. The term was first applied to Aristotle, I think. As the codifier of what the West – and given the expansionist fervor with which the West has tried to absorb the rest of the world in the last five hundred years, what the world – regards thinking to be, he deserves the honor, conferred with regret. Norman O. Brown, a great culture critic, thought that Freud was the master of those who know. For a long time my candidate was Dostoyevsky: hence the opening of these remarks. Heinrich von Kleist believed that we must eat twice of the fruit of the tree of knowledge: the imperative of the first time is that we learn from the masters of those who know; but the second time, the last time? Perhaps at the last we circle back to our mothers persuading us that the world can be trusted – by humming us to sleep.

Time^{Time}

Part 1

1.   The plurisubstantial order is a proper subset of the unisubstantial order.

1.1   The plurisubstantial order derives in the first instance from drawing a distinction.

1.11   The first consequence of persistence in drawing distinctions is a plurisubstantial world.

1.12   The second consequence of persistence in drawing distinctions is the hierarchizing of the plurisubstantial world.

1.121 The linguistic hierarchy in globally hierarchized plurisubstantial worlds is characterized by (1) univocal words, words with single referents, and (2) nested, asymmetrically ordered word-groups, constituting a hypotactic linguistic system.

1.122 The social hierarchy in globally hierarchized plurisubstantial worlds is characterized by unequal-outcome zero-sum, negative-sum, and positive-sum contests.

1.123 The spatial hierarchy in globally hierarchized plurisubstantial worlds yields diminishing foregrounds and expanded backgrounds.

1.124 The temporal hierarchy in globally hierarchized plurisubstantial worlds yields an increasingly articulated univocal past, a diminishing present, and the invention of a future.

1.2   The unisubstantial order derives in the first instance from erasing a distinction.

1.21   The first consequence of persistence in erasing distinctions is a unisubstantial world.

1.22   The second consequence of persistence in erasing distinctions in a world found to be plurisubstantial is the de-hierarchizing of that world, resulting in a unisubstantial world. No distinctions await erasure in an already unisubstantial world.

1.221 Words can express many meanings at once, they are polysemous, in a unisubstantial world. There is no linguistic hierarchy, but rather a paratactic linguistic antisystem.

1.222 Persons can express many aspects of themselves, they are polysemous, in a unisubstantial world. There is no social hierarchy, but rather communities of equi-valent persons connected through totemic identifications.

1.223 All entities in unisubstantial space are equi-valent: there are neither foregrounds nor backgrounds.

1.224 The moments in unisubstantial time that are most weighty are present moments. Little weight is given to a past, save for a kairotic polysemy in a non-univocal past – which polysemy is carried forward into the present, constituting much of its weight. There is no future: one "faces" the kairos.

Part 2

2.   What is the consequence of the plurisubstantial order being a proper subset of the unisubstantial order for the experience of time?

First, a stipulation: the two orders together, in this set-subset relation, make up most of what we mean by mentation.

Second, a more intuitive way of apprehending this set-subset relation.   In the plurisubstantial order, the mapping of a univocal word onto its single referent is a one-to-one map. In the unisubstantial order, the mapping of a polysemous word onto its several referents is a one-to-many map. The latter can then be seen as including the former. The type of word-map belonging to the order being synecdochal for the entire order, the whole of the plurisubstantial order is included in the unisubstantial order.

Rather than refer to the relative weights of moments in the two orders – weight concentrated in a univocal past and an invented univocal future in the plurisubstantial order, concentrated in a kairos-supported present in the unisubstanial order – let us look at (1) Henri Bergson's Heraclitean/evolutionary notion of an over-arching, ever-thickening "Duration," every past moment gathered into every ongoing present moment [Henri Bergson, *Creative Evolution,* trans. A. Mitchell, NY, Henry Holt and Company, 1911], and (2) Julian Barbour's Parmenidean/cinematic notion of a timeless universe-of-still-frames that are run as if by a movie projector, producing the illusion of time, a universe he calls "Platonia" [Julian Barbour, *The End of Time,* Oxford, Oxford University Press, 1999].

Variants of Becoming and Being like Duration and Platonia normally occupy poles on a continuum of conceptions of time. It may be the case, however, that "continuum" is the wrong metaphor. If we change the metaphor to "concentrism," one set situated as a proper subset of another set, and we continue with our stipulation about mentation, then it is an easy step to the suggestion that one can experience Bergson's ingathering time and Barbour's illusory time *simultaneously,* the latter a commonsense-time-free, element-rich cross-section of the former. The strain on non-contradiction is considerable, of course, and modernity, which is distinction-drawing, plurisubstantial, hierarchical, univocal, orderly, and contestual has subverted much of the polysemous order, so modern persons are likely to experience time as either thinly successive rather than densely so in Bergson's formulation, or thinly timeless rather than densely so in Barbour's. So let us bracket Aristotle, modernity, and the alternation "or," and instead imagine Bergson's formulation comfortably containing Barbour's, replacing the alternation with the conjunction "and." We are entirely capable of experiencing the world as manifesting evolutionary, ever-filling time *and* static, forever full time, at once.

Finally, one of the reasons language and society are taken up in Part 1 as well as time is that meditations on language and society might fruitfully submit to the manner of Part 2 regarding time.

Sublation

A

B

A+B   Addition: school

A

B

A*+B!   Pretentious addition: postmodern architecture

A

B

A+B=C   Transformation: French baking

A

B

AB=ABC   Brahms

www.ingramcontent.com/pod-product-compliance
Lightning Source LLC
LaVergne TN
LVHW081315060426
835509LV00015B/1516

9780615570372